Dog Training
FOR CHILDREN & PARENTS

Michael Tucker

Howell Book House

Howell Book House
A Simon & Schuster Macmillan Company
1633 Broadway
New York, NY 10019

Macmillan Publishing books may be purchased for business or sales promotional use.
For information please write: Special Markets Department, Macmillan Publishing
USA, 1633 Broadway, New York, NY 10019.

Copyright © 1998 Michael Tucker

MACMILLAN is a registered trademark of Macmillan, Inc.

Library of Congress Cataloging-in-Publication Data:
Tucker, Michael, 1934–
Dog training for children & parents/by Michael Tucker.
    p.   cm.
ISBN: 0-87605-583-8
1. Dogs—Training. 2. Dogs. 3. Children and animals. I. title.
SF431.T817 1998
636.7/0887—dc21   97-39653
     CIP

Manufactured in the United States of America

Text design by designLab, Seattle

Contents

Acknowledgments

I wish to express my sincere thanks to my friend, Jim Hopson, for his time, patience and expertise in taking all the photographs for this book. I also wish to thank everyone who readily agreed to be in the photographs. They include veterinarian Dr. Alison Brown B.V. Sc., (Hons.) MACVS, MRCVS and many young handlers, some accompanied by their parents, who have trained and willingly demonstrated with their dogs of various breeds. Some have been trained at my own dog training school, and some have been trained at Cogley's Top Dogs. I also wish to thank members of my own family for assisting me in so many ways and the Royal Guide Dogs Associations of Australia, whose two Labradors pictured herein were in our care for a few months at the time these photographs were taken.

Last, but by no means least, my grateful thanks to Dorothy Wellington who, once again, undertook the typing of the text and to Howell Book House for publishing this book.

Introduction

When I was a young boy living in England, most families had a dog and some had more than one. But I cannot remember ever seeing people train their dogs. This was not surprising really because they didn't know how to go about training like we do today. If people taught their dogs anything, the methods used were based very much on trial and error, hit or miss! Obedience dog clubs were virtually unheard of, and very few books about dogs contained little, if any, advice on the training of dogs.

There was little traffic on the roads in those days, some of which was horse drawn, so owners tended to let their dogs roam the streets during the day. Dogs who could not be trusted were kept inside their properties. Sadly, many of them were never taken out for walks, not even on a leash. That was a terrible existence for those poor dogs. Their owners should never have had them.

Then the second world war came. During those dreadful years, dog breeding was rare, which perhaps was a good thing. It is interesting to note, however, that a large number of adult dogs were offered to the Royal Air Force and the Army in which they were trained to carry out a number of tasks. During their years of service, a lot of those dogs saved many human lives, often working in times of great danger.

After the war, dog breeding started up again and an interest was shown in dog training. That interest continued to grow and the achievements gained in that field rose beyond all expectations.

There is a great responsibility in owning a dog, and therefore all dogs should receive basic training. Owners who have trained dogs openly declare what a pleasure it is to have well-behaved pets.

I started obedience training with my Collie when I was 16. I joined what was then one of the very few dog training societies in England. Fortunately, the club was only two miles away. The membership was very small in those days, and I was undoubtedly the youngest member. As the years passed by, dog training clubs increased in size and number, and as they did, it was pleasing to see more young people joining.

In the early sixties, younger children started to join the clubs, and some of them showed how they could train just as well as the adults. At the Stratford-Upon-Avon Dog Training Club, at which I was head trainer, we had a children's class once a week that was held in a community hall early in the evening prior to the adult classes. All the children, who had small dogs, did extremely well. The instruction they received put them in good stead to possibly train larger dogs when they became adults.

Children in many countries are becoming increasingly aware of dogs being trained for various types of work. Television has been largely responsible for this awareness, and of course more and more books have been written on the subject of dogs and their health, care and training. I find that, whenever I visit schools or children's organizations, children are most interested in knowing how a dog should be trained and are so attentive when they actually see my dog do the exercises. They ask most intelligent questions and always want to know more. Schoolteachers have often commented that they have never seen their classes so well behaved and attentive! The subject is so fascinating that it holds their interest too.

Since I set up my own training school and consultancy in 1975, I have been training more and more children with their dogs. Success is possible, provided that the children are big enough and strong enough to manage their dogs. But if their dogs are too large and strong, then I would suggest and expect their parents to train and control the dogs. However, I find that children are very good mimics! This is a great asset because they will need to copy the intonation of their instructor's voice if they are to get the best responses from their dogs.

It is always a great pleasure for me when some of those children come to me years later as adults with new dogs to train again. Many of them are married by this time, and some even have small children themselves. A few of them have taken up careers with dogs. I know of two former trainees who are veterinary surgeons. Another, whom I have known since the day she was born and who showed a natural rapport with dogs even as a small child, is now a qualified guide dog instructor. Others have taken up employment in numerous animal health shelters, and the list goes on.

PART 1
General Handling and Care of the Dog

Chapter 1
A FEW WORDS FROM A DOG

My name is Patch. No one knows my ancestry, but I am just one of millions of dogs who thought you might like to know about some of the things we enjoy most in life. I think the greatest thing we can share with human beings is true companionship. Naturally, we can't talk, but we can communicate with our owners in so many different ways.

We love daily walks; good, nourishing food to eat; a comfortable bed; a regular brush and comb and an occasional bath to keep us clean. We thoroughly enjoy meeting and romping with other dogs in the parks, chasing after a ball and bringing it back and playing with an assortment of toys at home that we get as birthday and Christmas presents and at other times. They are great fun to play with.

Training can be great fun, too. It gives us some work to do and prevents us from getting bored. All well-trained dogs are happy dogs for they are working so closely with their owners. What more could we ask for?

Like humans, we dogs are creatures of habit. We often amaze people with the things we do at certain times of the day. We also have an uncanny way of knowing things, which has simply mystified people for centuries. It is as if we have an inner sense that cannot be explained. We can sense all types of danger. We know those who love us and those who do not. We all have our ways of doing things. This can be seen from breed to breed. We've all been bred for different purposes.

Unfortunately, some dogs get a really bad deal—they're tied up all day, left in a backyard or constantly scratching because they get fleas on them that drive them mad. They hate being teased, screamed and shouted at; worse still, they hate being hit or having things thrown at them. Only ignorant, cruel, non-caring people treat them that way.

However, for all our needs to which our kind owners provide and the vets who do such wonderful work in caring for our health, we can give so much in return. We like giving comfort to the lonely, happiness to the sad, support and protection to those who need it, a calming effect on those with health problems and many more things. But the most treasured thing we can give is true companionship.

Your affectionate dog!
Patch

Chapter 2
BECOMING A DOG OWNER

Why Do You Want a Dog?

I believe that it is true to say that most people want a dog as a companion. And that reason alone is, I think, a most valid one. Others own dogs to serve as guards as well as companions, which is also a very good reason to have a dog. Some get purebred dogs whom they like to show. Some like to train their dogs for obedience competitions. But it upsets me to see or hear of people who get dogs purely to guard premises and for nothing else. Often those poor dogs become frustrated, aggressive and finally dangerous. They rarely receive proper care, and their living conditions are often deplorable. Worse than those people are the few who get dogs, like Bull Terriers and American Pit Bull Terriers, and then train the dogs to be aggressive or to engage in illegal dog fighting. This is a dangerous and cruel practice.

Choosing a Dog

Many children are fortunate enough to have a dog, but for those who are not so lucky, they often live in hope that one day their parents will allow them to have a dog of their particular choice. Making that choice is not always easy.

When choosing a dog from such a wide variety of breeds, an important first question for both children and adults is, "Are we big enough and strong enough to handle and train that particular breed of dog?" It is very easy for children to fall in love with a particular breed—they may have seen the dog in picture books, in films, on television or may actually know someone who has one. But children and their parents also need to find out how big, heavy and strong the desired dog will be when fully grown. Most herding and gun-dog breeds are quite trainable, but other breeds, like terriers and hounds, are more difficult to train.

If any purebred dog is chosen, it is advisable to find out as much as possible about that breed. For example, many people have chosen the Alaskan Malamute because he looks nice and he is very friendly with people. Although the breed does tend to have those qualities, many people choosing a Malamute do not know that the breed is difficult to get to come on command and that he can be aggressive to other dogs—especially to dogs living under the same roof.

As far as crossbred dogs are concerned, there is no guarantee as to how they are going to turn out. For example, I once trained a dog who was a cross between a Chow Chow and a Yellow Labrador. He really looked half and half! Now the Labrador Retriever is one of the easiest dogs to train, but the Chow Chow can be one of the most difficult dogs to train and can be unpredictably aggressive. Fortunately, the dog's temperament and working ability followed that of the Labrador. I anticipated problems if it had been the other way about.

Whatever type of dog people decide to get, whether it is a purebreed or a crossbreed, they will generally find that the female is easier to handle than the male dog. The female is more responsive and caring. She gives herself readily to her owner, like she does in looking after her young ones if she has any. That is

This handsome Keeshond would make a nice pet.

her maternal instinct. The male dog frequently wants to have his own way. He is often more distracted by everything around him, especially other dogs, and he is likely to be more difficult to control than the bitch. In choosing a suitable dog, children should be carefully guided by their parents, who will be expected to give a leading hand in rearing the animal.

Choose a Friendly Dog

You can purchase dogs and puppies from a variety of places these days. Most, particularly the purebred breeds, are purchased from breeders. Others are mainly from the shelters and rescue centers. From time to time, owners, realizing that they cannot keep their dog anymore, will place an advertisement in a newspaper and hope to find a good home for their dog that way. A few dogs are purchased from guide dog schools, police dog schools and customs dog schools. These dogs, which have been deemed unsuitable in those particular types of work, are usually dogs with great temperaments, but for some reason or other, they have not matched up to the school's requirements. As detailed records are kept on the dogs, purchasers of these pets can inquire as to why the dog has been rejected. But those up for sale in shelters and rescue centers are really unknown quantities. Often nothing is known of the dog's history and what his temperament is really like in the home. This cannot really be assessed in the kennels and runs. Some purchasers have been extremely lucky in selecting and purchasing a good dog at such centers, while, sadly, others have been most unfortunate—they have gotten a dog only to find that after a day or so he turns out to be aggressive. The chances are that he was aggressive in his former home, which is why and how he ended up in the pound, shelter or rescue center.

If you ever visit a breeder and observe a litter or two, look for good temperament first, not good looks. If he looks like the prettiest dog in the world yet is shy and hides behind his kennel, I would advise you not to select him, otherwise you could end up with much trouble on your hands. Don't be fooled by what the breeder might say in trying to assure you that everything will be all right. Over the years I have had many clients tell me that in a time of weakness, they felt sorry for the puppy or dog and selected him, only to later regret having taken him on.

If you do purchase a pedigree dog, be sure that you get the pedigree certificate and that it is complete in every respect and signed by the breeder in transferring ownership. Also make sure you get a receipt for your payment and the dog's inoculation certificate signed by the veterinarian. Never accept the word of a breeder who promises that all these papers will be sent to you in the mail. In my opinion, a reputable breeder will see that you have all those necessary papers at the time you make the purchase and take delivery of the puppy.

Be sure to choose a dog who is friendly and not aggressive in any way. But at the same time, do not choose a dog who is very docile. He is likely to become a very lazy dog! Look for a dog who is fairly active, one who is attentive, inquisitive and has a calm disposition. Select one who is bold and not afraid of you or anything around him. If he is a puppy, watch how he plays with his littermates. See how he listens to you when you make some quiet, interesting noises. If he cocks his head from side to side, it shows that he is interested. Then walk around slowly and see if he, and perhaps the whole litter, follows you. When you have selected the dog of your choice, whether he is a young puppy or an adult dog, you will need to give him a nice name, one that you feel everyone will like.

I shall always remember a lady who brought her 18-month-old German Shepherd bitch to me for assessment and training. She had owned the dog for one month. She saw that the dog was for sale in the newspaper. She telephoned the number, and the breeder brought her down from the country a few days later. He stayed in the house for about two hours, saying to the lady that he would only sell the bitch to her if the dog settled down with her. After a little longer he said how pleased he was that his dear dog had settled down with her.

The whole family will enjoy a friendly, unaggressive dog.

Then the lady asked the man how much he wanted for the bitch. He said, "Well, she is worth $1,500.00, but as I'm so pleased to see how she has settled down so well with you, madam, and I now know that you have a lovely home in which to care for her, I'll let you have her for $1,000.00 and I'll send all the papers to you in the mail tomorrow." Foolishly, she admitted to me, she paid him the $1,000.00 and that was the last she saw of him. Needless to say she never received the promised papers. If the truth was known, the breeder could have purchased the dog, for very little money, from the pound or even stolen the dog. That is one of many stories I can tell. So my advice to all purchasers of dogs is to be very careful and check everything out. If you sense anything suspicious happening, don't proceed any further, go elsewhere.

Do You Already Have a Dog at Home?

Another point that must be taken into consideration is whether another young or old dog already lives with you at home. Will your dog get on all right with the new dog you are getting? Unfortunately, there is no definite answer to that question. Generally, if you have a male and a female they should get on well together, but if you have two males or two bitches, then you could have problems. Dogs of the same sex may become jealous and fight. If you find that your two dogs won't live together happily, you may need to find another home for one of them.

Chapter 3
SETTLING YOUR PUPPY OR DOG INTO HIS NEW HOME

Preparing Your Home for a New Dog

If you live in a house and expect to allow your pet outside on his own, you must adequately fence your yard.

Secure Fences & Gates

Make sure all your fences are high enough to keep your dog enclosed (and other dogs out), and that gates are secure so your dog does not wander out onto the road and get injured or, worse still, killed by a passing vehicle. Whenever you go out through a gate, go out backwards so that you are facing the dog and in a position to prevent him from trying to get out. Dogs can be very quick, so you must not take any chances.

Give a Puppy Time to Get Acquainted With the New Home

When you have made the choice and brought your puppy home, it is the first big change in his life. Remember that he has left his mother, his littermates and the breeders who have cared for him.

It is important that a dog be able to see what is going on outside of the property.

Hold the dog back with one hand as you open and close the gate with the other.

At first your home will seem strange to your puppy. You will need to help him by making the change as pleasant as you can. (Adult dogs will also need a period of adjustment.) Talk to your puppy or dog a lot and make him feel really at home and wanted. Use a quiet, pleasant tone of voice as he walks around your backyard sniffing and investigating everything. Then take him inside and continue to use your voice to reassure him as he moves from room to room with you. Show your puppy his crate or bed and encourage him to explore his own personal area.

You will find it fascinating to watch your puppy looking at certain things and sometimes barking at them. As we all know, puppies' eyes do not open until they are about three weeks old. But even when you have brought your new puppy home at the age of, let's say, seven to eight weeks, his focal length of vision is not very long. However, his length of vision becomes longer as the weeks and months pass by. If he sees something at a distance that is just beyond focal length, it will not be clear to him as to what it is. This may worry him, and he'll start to bark at it. Then when that object or person comes nearer to him or he goes forward to investigate, everything comes into focus and your puppy is quite happy again. When a dog is fully grown, his focal distance is extremely great—he will focus on an aircraft in the sky several miles away. So watch how your puppy develops and how he uses his eyes.

It is quite amusing to see the reaction of a puppy or adult dog when he sees himself in a mirror for the first time. If the mirror is screwed to a wall, he will either look at his reflection curiously or even bark at it. Then he will go to the mirror and put his nose on it, only to find that there is no doggy smell to the other dog of the same breed—himself! He will then ignore it and will not be bothered with it again in the future.

This Golden Retriever puppy relaxes and shares the company of members of the family as they watch television.

When I was a guide dog trainer, I noticed that when I worked a guide dog in training through the clothes department of a large store where there were a number of full-length mirrors about 18 inches wide in the middle of the floor, the dog showed an interest in his reflection. I allowed him to walk up to the mirror to investigate, just because I was interested to see what would happen next. In the vast majority of cases, each dog, having sniffed the glass, walked around the back of the mirror, expecting, I guess, to find the other dog! Unable to find him, the dog then decided to carry on walking. In subsequent visits to these department stores, the dogs showed no interest in the mirrors at all. They were not going to be fooled a second time.

You may now ask whether a dog is able to understand and watch a television screen. Generally speaking, they don't, but there are a few who do. In many of those cases it is when the dog hears the sound of an animal. He looks up curiously, concentrates on the screen for a moment and ventures forward but then diverts slightly to one side and listens to the speaker. In other cases where there has been no sound, dogs have viewed other dogs on the screen when the image of the performing dog has been on a plain background.

While writing this chapter, however, I observed something with a six-month-old Miniature Schnauzer called Bertie that I wish to share with you. We were caring for him while his owners were overseas for two weeks. One day, our daughter, Sharon, brought her two Miniature Schnauzers to play with him in our backyard. At the same time, her young son, Matthew, had a little putt around with a golf ball. My wife recorded some of this with her video camera. About a week later, we viewed this on our television screen and were quite surprised to see how Bertie took so much interest. In fact, he stepped back a few feet, sat on the carpet and watched himself play with the other two. Naturally, we kept quite quiet as we didn't want to break his concentration. This went on for some time until the scene changed to where Matthew lined himself up to hit the golf ball, aiming it slightly to the left of the camera and out of the picture. As the white golf ball was projected, Bertie quickly followed it with his eyes as if it was coming out of the television set and into the room, but then Bertie sat there, mystified as to where the ball had gone. Bertie's viewing of the video clearly showed that he recognized the dogs running around on the grass and also Matthew hitting the golf ball, which he had chased after the week before. He was fascinating to watch, especially as he is only six months old.

A few days later our daughter, Alison, and I watched Bertie view the video recording again. As soon as he saw it, he took up the same position as before, about five feet in front of the television, which is situated in the corner of the room and just to the

Bertie enjoyed watching himself on television!

right of the large glass sliding door looking out on to the lawn in the backyard. He sat there most interested with ears erect and displaying the utmost concentration as he watched the dogs, including himself, play on the back lawn. Then we noticed him suddenly glance several times to the left to see if the dogs were in the backyard, but of course there was no movement at all, not even a bird at the time. These sudden glances lasted no more than a second each. All this showed that he remembered his doggy friends playing with him on the lawn. He watched the television screen, but he also wanted to make quick checks to see if the dogs were actually playing in the backyard.

Four days later his owner, Alison's mother-in-law, returned from her overseas trip to collect Bertie. Naturally, he was very excited to see her. When he had settled down we told her how he liked watching the television. She soon saw this when the video was shown. As before, he watched it and made a quick glance or two through the window to see if any of his pals were playing in the garden. Then curiosity must have really seized him because he walked over to the square fly-wire flap, stuck his head through, looked left then right and then hopped out to really check the backyard. Satisfied that there were no dogs outside, he quickly returned inside to watch the television screen again, during which time I took photos of him.

In all my years of living with dogs and training them, I have never made such interesting observations before in connection with dogs watching a television screen. Such things are fascinating, aren't they? I hope that you, my readers, will also enjoy such fascinating times as you watch your own dog's reactions to things like these from day to day.

Although the dog's number one sense is his sense of smell and his second sense is that of hearing, his third sense, sight, is most interesting to study. So watch your dogs use their eyesight, and read all you can on the subject. There's so much to learn.

Start Housebreaking Right Away!

Apart from showing your new pet both the inside and outside of your home, the most important thing is to begin housebreaking. This is quite simple if you go about it the right way. First of all, restrict your puppy to one or two rooms of the house so that you can keep a watchful eye on him. Don't let him have the complete run of the house, otherwise he might go to the toilet in various rooms without you knowing it until much later. Not only will you be kept quite busy cleaning up the mess, but it will become a dirty habit if he is allowed to do it in the wrong places. So you will need to take him outside regularly to a certain place in your backyard, either by carrying him or leading him there on a leash, and encourage him to go to the toilet by first using words like "Get busy" several times. As soon as he has finished, show how pleased you are by saying, "Good dog! Very good! Oh, you are a clever dog!" Note carefully that the praise should be given as soon as he has finished and starts to walk away. It is not advisable to praise him during the time that he is relieving himself. If you say, "Good dog!" when he is perhaps halfway through, he may suddenly leave off going to the toilet and come over to you, wagging his tail as if to say, "Am I really a good dog?" In so doing this, he might still have half a bladder full! So when he starts to relieve himself and continues, just keep saying slowly and quietly, "Busy! Busy!" as many times as is necessary until you actually see him cease to do anymore and walk away. Then you can praise him feeling fairly sure that he has emptied himself completely. Then bring him inside again. In quite a short time your dog will understand why you have taken him outside. And later, if you watch carefully, you will see him go to the back door. This is his way of telling you that he wants to go outside to do his business.

Naturally you can expect to have a few accidents in the home, very often on the carpet! If you catch your dog in the act, say "No!" and take him outside immediately and stay with him until he has finished outside. If you have discovered the accident some time after, it is too late to correct your puppy. Just clean it up thoroughly and watch the dog more closely in the future. Never scold the puppy by rubbing his nose in the mess. You will do more harm than good by treating your puppy in that way. Such treatment is likely to make the dog worried, and he will probably make more messes.

A few years ago, a five-month-old St. Bernard male puppy came to me for training. Every time he came he would have a good long wee on the grass. One day I decided to time him. Would you believe that his long wee lasted for 58 seconds!

With respect to an adult dog who has been selected from a shelter or rescue society, there may be no prior knowledge as to

*Every puppy should be taken out regularly to his familiar toilet ground. Be patient,
watch carefully and praise your puppy when he has relieved himself,
like this Miniature Schnauzer puppy.*

whether the dog has been housebroken. If he has, there should
be no problems, but if he hasn't, it could be harder or take longer
to teach him than to teach a puppy. This is because an adult dog
may have had a bad habit for a long time; it is difficult to break
that habit and create a new one. The puppy has not developed the
bad habit but is developing a clean habit right from the start.

Learning to Live Together

You will hear a lot of people say, "Our dog is one of the family!" This is always very nice to hear and it should be the case if we want the loyal companionship that dogs can and do give us. They also give us that sense of security in our homes. In return for the enjoyment our dogs give us we must see that they receive good food, clean drinking water, comfortable sleeping accommodations, daily grooming, baths when necessary, visits to the vet, gentle handling, basic obedience training, regular walks and many other things.

Get your dog used to being left on his own in the house. Don't take him with you wherever you go, because he will then expect to go with you at all times. The problem then arises, when you find it necessary to leave your dog on his own for several hours, that he barks and howls for attention all day until you return. This can be prevented if you start off by leaving your dog in the house for short periods, such as a quarter of an hour. Then as the days and weeks go by you can gradually increase the time you are away. Provided you have given your dog a walk beforehand, he will gradually get used to your absence, knowing that you will return.

Many years ago a friend of ours asked us if we would care for her black Labrador Retriever bitch for four weeks while she and her husband went away for a holiday in Queensland. She had always been in the habit of taking her dog with her wherever she went. Added to this, the dog slept in our friend's bedroom every night.

We agreed to care for her dog but made it quite clear that she would not be allowed in our bedroom but would share the laundry with our German Shepherd.

Well, on the first night when we went to bed, this Labrador started crying and scratching at the door. I jumped out of bed, went into the laundry and said, "Quiet!" Then I gave her a shake on the neck, put her in her basket again, shut the door and went to bed. Silence reigned for about 10 minutes, but then this bitch howled again, so I went into the laundry and corrected her again. I did not get much sleep that night because I was correcting her every half hour at least. It was a battle of the wills, and I was not going to give in.

The next night she howled within a few minutes of my leaving her in the laundry so I carried out the same correction. After that she made not a sound, nor did she do it anymore for the whole month she was with us. It was, therefore, worth losing one night's sleep in order to have a peaceful time for the rest of the month. When we told our friend of the success, she could not believe that it was possible. But the point I really wish to make here is that all that trouble could have been prevented if this dog had been brought up to accept that she had to be left on her own at times during the day and that she had to sleep elsewhere in the house at night. Otherwise the whole business can become a burden. Start as you mean to go on!

You may ask whether a dog should sleep in the house at nighttime or sleep in a kennel outside. For many reasons it is best to have the dog inside. A close bond can form between you and the dog. Because you are with him more, you can talk to him, train him, control him, introduce him to visitors and feel his close companionship. For your personal safety a dog can also protect you in your home and act as a deterrent in guarding your home when you are out.

If a dog is kenneled outside, he can be disturbed by things he sees and hears moving at nighttime, which will cause him to bark and in turn to annoy the neighbors. Your dog can get up to all sorts of mischief outside while you are asleep, and you won't be there to correct him. Your dog can be irritated by flies during the day and mosquitoes at night. He can get filthy in wet weather if he runs around the backyard day and night. From a security point of view, if your dog is in the backyard, he cannot protect you or guard your home if an offender were to break inside at the front of your house.

On balance it is much safer to have your dog inside, especially at nighttime. He is protected from bad weather and any possible harm from unfriendly people or animals who may venture onto your property. When you do leave your dog outside, it is preferable to provide him with a "run" or a compound, rather than tethering him. Tying a dog up can lead to an aggressive, angry pet.

Chapter 4
FEEDING

After a few days of settling in, you should start to teach your puppy to sit for his meals (see "Sit," page 99). This is very simple if you put him on the leash and collar. Doing so will help you to control your pet. When you have put his bowl of food on the floor, wait a few seconds, then bend down, point with your hand and say in a very pleasing voice, "You can have it!" And as he scampers to the food, praise him by saying, "Good dog!" You can then remove the leash. You could of course keep hold of it so that, as soon as the puppy has eaten all his food, you could lead him outside to do his toilet. In many cases, when a dog has finished eating he will want to go to the toilet. He will also want to go when you both get up every morning and before going to bed at night. Of course, you may need to take your dog out during the middle of the day—puppies tend to need a visit outdoors quite frequently.

Your vet will be able to advise you as to how often you should feed your dog and as to the type and amount of food that is best.

If you hand-feed a dog, offering him, let's say, a dog biscuit, never let him snatch it out of your hand. Hold the biscuit firmly and say, "You can have it." If it is taken gently, there won't be a

Teach your dog to sit for his meal until told to eat. Ensure that the dog has fresh drinking water at all times.

problem. But if the puppy snatches it, pull it away and don't let the puppy have it. Then offer it once again, saying in a quiet, slow voice, "Gently! Gently!" You might have to do this a few times, but when the puppy decides it is better to take the biscuit gently, let him have it and say in a quiet, slow voice, "Good dog." He will soon learn that he can take something from your hand only if he takes it gently.

25

When having a meal at the table, allow your dog to relax, but never feed him from the table.

It is a bad idea to feed your dog bits and pieces from the table. Once you start doing so, your dog will keep bothering you and other people who come to your house for a meal.

Allow Your Dog to Eat in Peace

When you feed your puppy or adult dog, allow him to eat his meal in peace. Don't disturb him. Some dogs become quite snappy when they are eating, and they often become like this because they have been disturbed. Some people try taking the dog's food bowl away when he is about halfway through his meal. Although some dogs put up with this, others become very annoyed, which is understandable. Imagine yourself, as a child or adult, halfway through eating a delicious meal in a restaurant when a rude waiter walks over to your table, sits down beside you to watch you eat, patting you on the head perhaps, and then, without any warning, suddenly takes your plate away without a word of explanation. Wouldn't you be furious? Who wouldn't be? Customers would soon be asking for the waiter to be sacked for his outrageous behavior. So think about it that way and try to see it from the dog's point of view.

Discourage others outside your family from feeding your dog tidbits, whether he is in your own home or somewhere else to where you have been invited with your dog. I say this for two reasons: First, if he is allowed too many treats, your dog could very easily put on weight. When this happens, it is often very hard to slim the dog down again. Second, your dog will expect to be fed by other people and will therefore make a nuisance of himself by giving an appealing look as if to ask, "Have you got any for me?" drooling saliva from his mouth, nudging with his nose, scratching with a front paw or even barking to attract attention. I think the most polite and tactful way that you can deal with this is to thank people for their good intentions but hasten to add that your dog is on a special diet and you therefore respectfully request that your dog is not fed. Whenever I have been invited with my dog to give a talk to a large group of people and am then invited to stay for refreshments, I have made such an announcement and I have always found that my request has been met and the audience appreciates the request being made before tea is served.

It is best not to disrupt your dog when he's eating.

Water

Besides feeding the right type of food to your dog, always ensure that he has fresh drinking water. Clean the water dish and refill it with fresh water every day. Have one water bowl outside and another inside the house.

Chapter 5
GROOMING

You should groom your dog every day in order to keep him clean and healthy. If you have a short-coated dog, like a Boxer, you will only have to use a brush, but if you have a dog with a longer coat, like a Border Collie, you will need to use a steel comb and a brush. If you have a small breed, it is often easier to groom him on top of a table in the backyard; with a larger dog, it is often easier to groom him on the ground. Most dogs just love being groomed, and, after a few days, as soon as your dog sees you with the comb and brush in your hand, he will know that he is about to have his daily groom.

A few dogs fool around a bit when being groomed. If yours happens to be like that, it would be best for you to put him on the leash so that you are able to better control him. You will have a great opportunity to use the word "Stand!" when you are grooming your dog. Don't worry if he then decides to sit or lie down, just put your hand under his belly and gently and quietly say, "Stand!" and lift him up. As your dog stands up, praise him. Later, you will need to brush underneath his body. This is where you can tell your dog to lie down and then use the extra word, "Roll-over!" As you gently roll your dog onto his side, quietly praise him. It does not really matter what time of the day you wish to groom your dog. Some people like to do it during the early part of the day; others prefer the evening so that the dog feels comfortable as he goes to bed.

Brushing

Start grooming your dog by brushing his coat up in the opposite direction to which it grows. This helps to get rid of much of the loose dead fur and specks of dirt that any dog tends to pick up. Then comb the coat through from nose to tail, and finally brush it the same way.

When using a steel comb on the coat, be careful that you do not pull the comb against long hairs that have become knotted. Comb out the ends of the knotted hairs first, just as you would do with your own hair. You know how it can hurt when you quickly comb your hair and the comb pulls against hairs stuck together, don't you? Well, it will hurt your dog in just the same way. Some dogs, when hurt like this, have been known to turn around and bite the person combing them. So remember, comb with care.

Certain breeds have extremely fine hair that tangles in no time. With such dogs it is a good idea to groom them twice a day in order to prevent knots from developing in the coat.

In 1978 I trained a lovely crossbred dog with a shaggy coat for the stage musical *Annie*, which ran for nearly a year at Her Majesty's Theatre in Melbourne. I had to groom her twice a day to prevent her coat from becoming tangled because it was so fine and fairly long. So I groomed her every morning, then again when I arrived at the theater in the evenings. If I did not groom her for one or two days, then I had to spend far more time combing out all the knots. So by grooming most regularly, much time can be saved.

When you groom your dog every day, it gives you a very good chance to inspect your dog's entire body. Under his coat,

Take great care when combing out any knots in your dog's coat. Avoid hurting the dog by pulling on matted lumps of hair.

you may find different kinds of skin trouble, such as eczema or cuts. You may also discover fleas, lice or ticks. If long-coated dogs are not groomed every day, their coats can become so matted that it becomes impossible to comb out the knotted lumps of fur. It then becomes necessary to cut them off, which is not always easy when the fur is knotted so close to the skin. So make work easy for yourself by grooming daily.

Bathing

During the hot summer months, it is necessary to bathe your dog every two or three weeks—bathe them less frequently as the weather becomes colder. Oddly enough, most dogs don't really like being bathed. In fact, when they hear and see you preparing

*A spray hose on the tap is very useful to thoroughly rinse the shampoo
out of the dog's coat.*

to give them a bath, they know what is going to happen. Then,
when you say, "Would you like to have a bath?" they make a hasty
retreat and hide. However, when you get them into the bath,
shampoo them all over and thoroughly rinse them, they don't
seem to mind. It is advisable to consult your vet about what type
of shampoo and flea rinse you should use when bathing your
dog. Some shampoos could be too strong on certain dogs with
sensitive skins.

When the bath is all over, dogs shake a lot of the water out
of their coats and love being dried with clean towels. It is best to
choose a warm, sunny day and take your dog for a brisk walk in

Most dogs love being towel-dried.

the sun afterwards to dry out the rest of his coat. Avoid bathing your dog on a cold day because he could easily get chilled and become ill. As you are about to dry your dog, say, "Would you like to be dried?" As time goes on, he will understand that phrase and enjoy coming to you to be dried. If your dog ever becomes mischievous, say to him, "Do you want a bath?" and on hearing the word "bath," he will probably slink off into a corner and behave himself! These words and phrases become quite useful at times, don't they? When a dog comes out of a bath, he will naturally shake himself to get rid of a lot of the water in his thick coat. Just as he is about to do this, say, "Shake yourself!" and as he shakes, praise him by saying, "Good dog!" So there's another phrase you can say to your dog. You need to be quick in saying it. It is no good saying it after he has done it. Some dogs have been known to shake themselves on the command, "Shake yourself!" even when they are perfectly dry. Much depends on how many times the dog has had a bath, come out of the sea or gotten wet on other occasions. Obviously, the more times the dog has gotten wet and had to shake, the easier it is for the dog to learn the command. So try it and see how you go.

Chapter 6
LEASHES & COLLARS

Wearing a Collar

Waste no time in getting your dog used to wearing a leather collar. If you put it on for about 10 minutes several times a day, it is surprising how soon the dog will get used to it. Then keep it on for much longer periods of time and also attach to it an identification tag. On the tag, you should have your phone number or address, or both. Don't put your dog's name on the tag because if your dog is ever stolen, the thief would have the good fortune of knowing your dog's name.

With modern technology, many dogs are now having micro-chips inserted under their skin. These can be scanned with a special instrument to identify the dog. Ask your veterinarian about this means of identification.

The Leash

Your leash should be at least 4 feet (1.3 meters) long. Leather leashes are considered the best, but webbing or nylon leashes are also good. The leash should have a good, strong snap hook on the end that is easy to clip on to the ring of the collar. It is

Get your dog used to wearing a leather collar with suitable identification tags.

not wise to take a dog for a walk on a chain leash as this will hurt your hands whenever you need to correct your dog with a jerk.

Get your dog used to walking on the leash by doing it for very short periods of time as you walk around your backyard. Try to make it really fun by talking to your dog joyfully as you walk along, keeping the leash just slack. Avoid pulling it tight as this might make the dog panic and he will scream and attempt to pull away from you. With some dogs, you have to let go of the

Get your dog used to walking on the leash within your property before you take him out.

leash and let them drag it along on the ground as you continue to walk. In most cases, you will see the dog automatically follow because he is anxious to be with you. When this happens, show the dog how pleased you are by giving him lots of nice praise. Make the dog feel as if it is great fun and then pick up the leash as the dog trots along happily beside you.

Now you are probably wondering why I advise that your leash should be 4 feet long. There are several reasons for this. When you walk your dog freely on the leash, he should be given sufficient space around you in which he can be at ease. If your leash was shorter, or you wound a 4-foot leash around your hand a few times, you would restrict your dog. Not only would this make your dog frustrated and cause him to pull, but you might accidentally tread on your dog's hind feet if he suddenly walked in front of you.

If your dog saw something that he was not sure about, he would naturally become suspicious and attempt to pull away from it. If restricted, his slight fear would get worse and he would panic.

Another dreadful fault could arise if the dog was always on a very short leash. If a dog had even a small amount of protective-ness in his nature, he could develop protective aggression just because he was very restricted and held very close to his handler.

You will also need a long leash in obedience training, espe-cially when you want to teach your dog to stay while you move a few feet away from him. You certainly would not be able to move very far away holding a short leash. I shall explain more about this "Stay" exercise later in this book.

Last, a long leash will give you more leverage to lean back-wards when and if you have to control and correct your dog if he suddenly pulls forward with great force. If you had him on a short leash, he would cause you to lean forward as he pulled. You could so easily be pulled over flat on your face or you would be running after him— one or the other— with possible disas-trous results. I shall always remember when a young lady came to me for training many years ago with her powerful yellow Labra-dor Retriever. He was a bit short in the leg and she was six feet tall. She had him on an 18-inch leash. He pulled her quickly and with great force up my drive, accelerating with every yard they covered. It looked most dangerous. As they reached me, I grabbed his leash and caught her just in time before she could have had a nasty fall. I then put the dog on a 4-foot leather leash and explained everything to her. From that time on, the young lady found that it was so much easier to walk and train her dog on a long leash. As a matter of fact, she left her old short leash with me as she really had no further use for it. I still have it in my box of dog training equipment. I often use it when I am giving talks on dog training by showing it to audiences and explaining how and why it is so bad, and I go on to tell people the bad effects it can create. In my opinion, short leashes for dogs should never be made. I have seen so many problems arise with people's dogs when they are on short leashes. Naturally, the dog owners cannot really be blamed for buying these short leashes in the first place. How are they to know what problems may be ahead if they lead their dogs on them, unless they are advised by a trainer like myself or they read about them in a book like this one?

Always take great care of your leash. Never leave it lying around somewhere where your dog can get it and chew it, sometimes into several pieces! Avoid hanging your leash on a hook as many dogs will attempt to chew the end hanging down against the wall. It is much safer to roll the leash up neatly and put it in a drawer so that you know where it is and you can get it out quickly, especially in cases of emergency.

When you walk your dog on a leash, never allow him to grab hold of it in his mouth. Some dog owners think this is very funny and clever, but it isn't. When a dog bites his leash he is expressing that he wants his own way. This must be corrected immediately with a firm "No!" followed by a quick, short jerk on the leash. As soon as he responds by releasing his grip on the leash, praise him slowly and quietly.

Quite a number of people, who have come to my school for training, have their dogs on leashes that are knotted together and have sections that have been clearly bitten halfway through. Leashes in these chewed conditions are positively dangerous. One jerk on the leash or a sudden, strong, unexpected pull by the dog could snap the leash in two, and the dog could run off into the road and be injured. Such an event could cause a serious accident. So always make sure you have your dog on a good leash.

Avoid purchasing shiny nylon leashes. They are so smooth that you will find them hard to grip without them slipping through your hand. The webbing leashes are much better.

The only use I would have for a chain leash would be for when I had to tether a dog to a pole for a short length of time. He could not chew through a chain leash, whereas he could easily chew through a leather leash tied to a pole and run off with disastrous results.

Always remember that your leash and slip-chain collar is your equipment of control. It has a handle at one end and a clip at the other, and it is 4 feet long. To control the dog and teach the dog the various exercises, it has to be held correctly and kept slack. Also, the jerks you make with it should be kept to a minimum. Such corrective jerks on the leash must be given at the correct angle and height of the dog. The corrective jerks should be given as soon as the dog starts to misbehave or make an error. As soon as the dog responds favorably, the leash should be relaxed immediately and quiet, slow, vocal praise given.

The amount of force you need to apply when giving a corrective jerk depends not on the weight, strength and size of the dog, but on the sensitivity of the dog's body. Some dogs are highly sensitive and therefore need only a little jerk to make them respond. Other dogs are very tough and therefore require a much firmer corrective jerk for it to be effective. So you have to work out how sensitive the dog is in order to apply the appropriate amount of force. If, for example, you gave a highly sensitive dog a very hard corrective jerk, he would not be able to cope with such a correction. Conversely, if you gave a little corrective jerk to a very tough dog, it would be totally ineffective.

With regard to slip-chain collars, which are also known as training collars, correction collars and choke collars, they come in various lengths, gauges and weight. With medium to large dogs, I would always recommend the long-linked collars. They have a better correction power, therefore you should not have to give many corrective jerks. With long-coated and semi–long-coated dogs, these long-linked collars, which are commonly called fur savers, do not cut the dog's fur down the right side of the dog's neck as the fine, small-linked collars tend to do. You will find that nearly all the professional dog training establishments throughout the world favor the long-linked slip-chain collar. For smaller dogs, the common small-linked collars are appropriate. But when purchasing one of these, it is advisable to spend a bit of money on a good one. Avoid buying a cheap one on sale in a supermarket. The quality is poor and they snap too easily. They are cheap in price and cheap in quality. You cannot afford to have one that will break, resulting in your dog possibly running into the road and getting injured.

There are also rolled leather slip collars and flat nylon slip collars. Both of these are ideal for dogs, usually little ones, that are highly sensitive. These collars are not so severe as the chain collars.

Whatever the slip collar is made of, make sure that it is not too long. It should be long enough to comfortably fit over the broadest part of the dog's head when you put it on and also when you take it off.

Slip-Chain Collars

I've had some clients bring their dogs to me on slip-chain collars that are far too long. Jokingly, I say, "Oh, dear! You've got a slip-chain collar on your dog long enough on which to swing an elephant!" Surprisingly, some people have the idea that when a long collar is jerked, the chain makes enough noise, as it goes through the round ring, to convey to the dog that it is a correction. Of course, this is not true. The dog responds to the actual physical jerk he feels on his neck, not the sound of the chain.

Most dogs, when they reach the age of about 14 weeks, need to be walked on slip-chain collars, which makes handling much easier.

You will need to know how to make up the slip-chain collar and the correct way to put it on your dog. By holding one of the rings horizontally in one hand, drop the rest of the chain collar through that ring with the other hand. Clip the leash onto the other ring. Practice putting the collar on your left wrist, imagining that it is your dog's head on your left side and you are facing the same way. Put it on so that the fine links, coming from the clip end of the leash, go through the round ring and continue *over* the top of the dog's neck. You will now find that, if you have to give a corrective jerk upwards with the leash, the chain collar will tighten; when you relax the leash, the chain collar will loosen automatically. However, if the slip-chain collar is put on the other way, so that the fine links go through the ring and continue *under* the dog's neck, the collar will certainly tighten when the leash is jerked upwards, but the collar will not loosen at all when the leash is relaxed.

Now you will probably want to know why dogs are trained to walk at heel on the handler's left side. Dog handling and obedience goes back many years. It first originated from the days man hunted with his dog and gun. Generally, he carried his gun in his right hand. Therefore, he put his dog on his left side so that the dog would not get in the way of the gun.[1] You will find that wherever you travel in the world today, all trained dogs, including dogs in the show ring, are heeled on the left. However, a few dogs are trained on the right. These dogs are frequently owned by disabled people who have lost their left arms. Here's a question for you: How would those few dogs have their training collars put on?

The author shows how to thread up a slip-chain collar.

Whatever you do with your dog every day, talk to him not only using single words of command but short sentences, too. For example, when you have decided to take your dog out for a walk, say, "Would you like to go for a walk?" Close to feeding time, say, "Would you like to have your dinner?" He will soon get to know the meaning of the word "walk" as you put him on his

Practice putting the collar on your left wrist as if it were your dog's neck. This is correct.

This way is incorrect, as the chain collar will not loosen when the leash is relaxed.

leash and collar and of the word "dinner" as you prepare his meal. When you say, "Would you like to have a brush?" your dog will soon know you are going to groom him as you walk toward the grooming table with the brush and comb in your hand. The huge number of words and phrases our dogs get to know is amazing. When you live so closely with a dog, he watches you, he gets to know your daily routine and he is constantly listening to you, though he may appear to be sound asleep.

Always eager to go for a walk, dogs soon learn how to put their noses into chain collars if held like this.

Many decades ago there was an old theory in dog training that all words of command should be short words of one syllable and that the number of commands should be kept to about 15. It was thought that a dog would not be able to cope with any more than that number. But as dog training has progressed over the years, that old theory is history. Dogs can learn many more commands and phrases as well. Perhaps the working dogs who possess the greatest vocabulary are the guide dogs for the blind, as they have to know, in addition to all the commands they are taught in their four months of training, a multitude of names relating to places where they frequently have to go, for example, names of shops, offices, homes and other places.

Here is a little trick that you can teach your dog to get him to put his chain collar on. Having said, "Would you like to go for a walk?" hold the collar in your left hand and encourage your dog to put his nose through the chain collar, through which he can see your right hand quietly flicking your thumb and finger. As your dog comes up behind you on your left side, say, "Put your collar on!" and as his nose goes through the collar, which you are holding quite still, give quiet praise, "You clever dog, very good!" You can also put your head down so that, as your dog is coming toward the collar, he can see your face through it.

[1]*In the past, guns were generally made for right-handed people. Naturally, left-handed people found them difficult to operate, especially bolt action rifles. However, some guns were made to order for left-handed shooters.*

Chapter 7
DAILY EXERCISE

Dogs are energetic animals and need exercise every day. However, before you take your puppy out to the streets, be sure that he has at least had his first set of inoculations. He may have had more than one set, depending on his age. If these have not been given, contact your veterinarian, who will provide this service and give any further advice about inoculations.

Walking Your Dog

When you take your puppy or adult dog for a walk every day, allow him to walk freely on the leash for most of the time. That means he can walk on your left or right, in front of you or behind. In fact, he is free to walk anywhere around you, and you can transfer the handle of the leash from one hand to the other as you walk along. As he walks along in that circular area around you, he can do as he likes within reason. But it is not within reason for him to pull hard on the leash; jump up at people, including yourself; or bark at and try to chase after dogs, cats, cars, joggers or anything else. It is all right if your dog has a quick sniff at the ground as he walks, but don't stop for him to have a sniffing session on a tree or post, otherwise he could keep

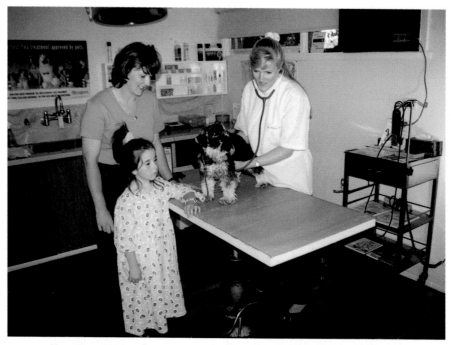

Your vet will be happy to give advice regarding the health and care of your dog.

you there for ages! Instead, keep walking, say, "This way!" and give a forward tug on the leash. Say in a pleasing voice, "Good dog!" as he obeys. Show the dog that you are the boss, that you are taking him for a walk and that you are not going to be detained.

You can also use "This way!" whenever you want to change direction on your walk. Once again, you might have to give him a little tug on the leash, but be sure to praise him with "Good dog!" as soon as he responds by following you.

As you go together down the street, walk slowly and talk quietly and slowly in order to keep the dog calm. If you hurry and speak quickly and loudly, you are likely to excite your dog; if he is a puppy, you could accidentally tread on him if he unexpectedly darted in front of you.

When out for a walk, allow your dog to walk freely on the leash for most of the time.

Sometimes dogs develop a habit of walking round and round you as you walk along. This continuous encircling pattern becomes a most annoying habit because you will be forever changing the leash from one hand to the other in front of you and behind you. So that's not much fun, is it?

This bad habit is easy to correct. As soon as your dog attempts to pass on your right side to walk around the back of you, stop him and turn him around for him to walk forward on your right side. You can do the same thing if the dog attempts to pass you on the left to go around the back of you.

Hold the leash high enough so that the puppy or dog can turn around at any time without getting his legs tangled in the leash. Keep the leash just slack. Don't pull it tight or else the dog will pull more.

Apart from the dog having a fairly good sized backyard or large property of a few acres in which to run around, he still needs to be taken out for a walk at least once a day. Always have your dog on a leash when you are on a road, even a quiet road. You never know when the odd vehicle will drive by.

If you can take your dog to a safe area, like a park or even on a beach (somewhere where he is safe and away from traffic), let him have a free run off the leash. As he runs around, just walk moderately slow and share in his fun by talking to him. Try suddenly changing your direction. Watch the dog and you'll see him come running after you. As he does so, say, "Good dog!" You will certainly keep him guessing as to which way you are going, and he will learn to keep an eye on you.

Another little thing you can do in order to make your dog follow you is to occasionally hide behind something like a big tree trunk. When you do, be sure that you can see him. When he realizes that you are not in his sight, he may run in your direction to find you, whereupon you should praise him when he finds you. On the other hand, he may stay in the same spot and keep looking in many directions. You will then see by his actions and the way he looks that he is starting to get worried. As soon as you see this anxiety, you should give him a call, "This way, boy!" This will restore his confidence. As he comes to the sound of your voice, praise him. If you were not to observe him nor give that reassuring call, he might panic and run in completely the opposite direction, possibly out of your sight, and become

It is most important that dogs have free runs in safe areas and are allowed to socialize with others.

hopelessly lost. Then you would be most upset and wish that you had never taken your eyes off him nor remained silent. So watch him carefully and never let him get worried about losing you.

Remember you said, "This way!" when you wanted to change direction as you walked your dog on the leash? Well, you can say "This way!" when you wish to change direction when you are free running him off the leash in a large, safe area. He will soon understand that "This way!" means that you require him to go in reasonably the same direction in which you are going, even though he may be several yards from you. Once again, praise him as soon as he responds.

If you do have more than one dog to free run in a park, it is always advisable to have one on the leash with you. With that one linked to you, the other dog or dogs will generally follow. If you let both or all your dogs off the leash, you might have great difficulty in getting them back to you. When I was a guide dog trainer, I would have up to eight dogs to train daily. I would always keep one on the leash while the others ran around freely in a large paddock. I would then call one and put him on the leash and let the other off to play with the rest. By rotation, each dog was with me on the leash while the others played. This method was most successful until they were all highly trained.

Free exercise for dogs is very important. If they do not get it, they can so very easily put on extra weight. When this happens, they feel it is a real effort to run free, so they just walk around putting on more weight. A similar thing happens with human beings.

I well remember a black Labrador who at the age of about 18 months weighed approximately 70 pounds. Then he started putting on more and more weight because of lack of exercise, and the owner gave him more to eat to satisfy his greedy appetite. He reached the enormous weight of 106 pounds. He was unable to run with other dogs, and it was an effort to walk far. Because he was too heavy, he was unable to jump into the car. He had to be lifted in.

Under veterinary care, the dog was put on a special diet and his weight reduced to 72 pounds over the next few months. During that time, he exercised more and more, ran around with other dogs again and was also able to jump into the car as he used to in the past. So the moral of this story is: Give your dog regular exercise, don't overfeed him and weigh him regularly—let's say every month—and keep a record of his weight.

When dogs get bigger, stronger, heavier and faster, you really have to watch carefully. When they are running around and after each other in great excitement, they can so easily run into you accidentally and quite unexpectedly. It is most unfortunate when a person has been accidentally knocked over by a dog who may be one of the friendliest you could ever wish to meet. So take great care and watch for other dogs, especially when they come racing up behind you.

For a puppy, the important thing is for him to meet people and get used to seeing, hearing and investigating things in the outside world. When he grows up, he will still need to be taken out, so that he does not become bored or frustrated by being kept at home all the time.

You should not walk a puppy too far when he is very young, otherwise he will become exhausted. Remember, his bones and muscles are growing and he will soon become tired, just like we all did when we were very young.

Although a puppy may be very energetic, do not run with him on the leash. In fact, it is better for you to walk slowly. The reason for this is that puppies often dash from side to side in front of us, quite unexpectedly at times, and we must be very careful not to tread on them. By walking slowly you have a much better chance of avoiding such frisky puppies. But if you run, you won't have much chance of avoiding your puppy if he suddenly cuts in front of you. Not only can the puppy be injured, like having his leg broken, but he can also become afraid of your great clumsy feet.

Managing a Frightened Dog

When out with your pet, you will pass many things that may appear to be strange and threatening to your dog or puppy; his natural reaction will be to move away from those things. If you allow that to happen without trying to help him overcome his fears, your dog or puppy will get worse and never want to go up to such things. When you see him become frightened or unsure about a particular object, let him out on the full length of the leash so that he can feel free to move around in a fairly large

circular area around you. This is known as the dog's area of
independence. This will help the dog, particularly a puppy, to
feel more at ease and give him time to settle down and overcome
his fears. Don't pull the leash tight or shorten it, otherwise the
dog will start to panic. Now start talking to and examining the
object by slowly running your hands over it. Very soon your dog
or puppy, thinking that he is missing out on something, will
gradually come up to it, sniff it and probably start wagging his
tail and thinking the whole thing is great fun. I have often
turned to my client and said, "Your dog feels unsure about the
ticking water meter," or, "That green garbage bag bellowing in
the breeze is disturbing your dog. Have you ever spoken to such
things before?" With an astonished look on his or her face, my
client declares in a somewhat uneasy way, "No, I haven't!" "Well,"
I reply, "Now's your chance!" I demonstrate first and then ask
him or her to do it by quite simply talking in a reassuring man-
ner while slowly running his or her hands over the object.
Within a very short time, the dog investigates the object and the
owner realizes the importance of the exercise. While you are
examining the object, talk to your dog by saying something like,
"Oh! What's this then? You have a look at this. That's very good.
Oh, you clever little dog! There now, isn't that cool, huh?" Now
take your dog a few steps back up the sidewalk, turn around and
walk by that object again; talk encouragingly as you do this. See
how your dog thinks it is great fun. There he is, wagging his tail.
He's not afraid anymore, is he? And why isn't he afraid? It is
because you have supported your dog and carefully introduced
him to such things so that he is quite happy about meeting them
again in the future.

You can use the same procedure when introducing your
dog or puppy to other dogs he may meet in the street. As you
approach the other dog, talk quietly and reassuringly. By doing

If your dog shows fear of any strange object, examine it and encourage your dog to meet it.

this, not only will you support your dog or puppy, but you can also have a calming effect on the strange dog. Keep your leash just slack but on the high side so that your dog doesn't get his legs over it. As the dogs sniff each other and revolve around, you must walk around, too, so that you are always on the opposite side to where the other dog is. Never let the other dog come between you and your dog. If there was a fight, you would not be able to pull your dog away. You will probably see the hackles come up on the necks, backs and tails of the dogs. This is not a sign of aggression, but a sign of caution. Each dog doesn't know what to expect of the other. With calm talking you can get them to relax and you will see the hackles come down. The tails will then wag freely, and the dogs will want to play.

Avoiding Pulling

The most common problem people have when walking their dogs is that their dogs pull. This does not make the walk very enjoyable. To stop the dog from pulling, say in a quiet, slow voice, "S-t-e-a-d-y!" Give the dog a quick jerk backwards and immediately relax the leash and stand still. You will notice him suddenly look around in surprise. As soon as you see this, praise quietly and slowly, "G-o-o-d d-o-g!" Then invite him to walk on again, "On you go! G-o-o-d d-o-g!" Repeat the correction every time he pulls. Later he will hear you say "S-t-e-a-d-y!" and will slow up immediately. When your command is obeyed as quickly as that, there will be no need for you to jerk the leash back. But don't forget to praise. Remember, talk quietly and slowly. With adult dogs who have developed the habit of pulling, be prepared to give a firmer jerk and do it immediately when the dog starts to pull. Old habits often take longer to cure, so be quick, consistent and patient.

Encountering New People

Some puppies and even adult dogs can be a bit shy when they meet people coming toward them on the sidewalk. So you need to support and encourage your dog to meet people in a friendly way. You could say to your puppy something like this: "Look! Who's that? Would you like to say hello? Go on then, you may say hello nicely. There's a good dog! That's right! You say hello nicely, but you must not jump up. Gently now, gently!" Then you should also greet the person politely, by saying, "Good morning, Sir (or Madam)!" and explain that, although you have not had your dog or puppy for very long, you are training him to be friendly and well behaved with everyone. When people see and hear you speak to your dog like that as you approach and meet them, they should feel so much more at ease, knowing that your dog is friendly, and should therefore admire the good work that you are doing.

To correct pulling on the leash, say "Steady!" jerk back and relax the leash immediately.
Praise slowly and quietly as you stand still, then move on again.

Unfortunately, many people greet a dog by putting their hands over the top and around the back of the dog's head. This can make a dog very shy and fearful, causing him to perhaps snap at the person. They should allow the dog to sniff their hand first, then stroke the dog under the chin. This will give the dog confidence. Now you do not always have the time to explain all that, and even if you did, some of those people still would not understand.

However, you can introduce your dog to the person or persons by asking, "Would you like to meet my dog by stroking him underneath his chin down toward his chest, because that is where he likes it best?" As you say this, demonstrate with your own hand on your dog how you would like them to do it. Nearly every time you say, "This is where he likes it best," they reply, "Is it?" Then they stroke him as you have demonstrated and requested, and everything is quite all right.

Take every opportunity to introduce your dog to people on the street.

If for any reason, your dog does snap at a person, correct him immediately by saying, "No!" and giving the dog a gentle jerk on the leash. Then invite him up to the person again. If his behavior is good, praise the dog quietly and slowly. The person will then be able to see that you are teaching the dog to behave himself and that you are making every effort to get the dog to be friendly.

It is amazing how introducing your dog to people you meet will lead to a very interesting conversation. When it is time to say, "Good-bye," always remember to thank those kind people for stopping to meet your dog and giving you their time. The next time that you meet those people on the street or in the park, not only will your dog recognize them, but they will be very happy to talk to you and your dog again.

Running Errands With Your Dog

It is not wise to tie your puppy to a pole outside a shop. When this is done, the puppy is very much on his own. You are not there to give him confidence. Because he can hardly move, he is likely to panic if he is frightened by something.

He could also feel very threatened if other dogs or teasing children came near him. He might then start to snap in order to protect himself.

Therefore, it is best for one person to have the puppy or dog on the leash outside the shop, while another member of the family goes inside to shop.

Getting Used to Traffic

You will also need to get your puppy or dog used to traffic. Your dog has possibly seen some vehicles drive past your property, which is a very good start. When you take your dog for a walk and you hear and see a vehicle coming up behind you, always play safe and stop for a while and let your dog turn around to watch the vehicle proceed along the street. Talk quietly all the time to assure that everything is all right and that there is nothing to worry about. You could easily say, "What's this coming along? There, look at that. You are a good dog. There it goes. Very good. Let's walk on now." By saying such nice things, you are sharing your lives together and forming a close bond. When you approach a busy main road, it is best for you to stop a short distance away so that all the vehicles going by appear to the dog to be at his own height. Crouch down and view the traffic yourself from the dog's eye level and you will understand what I mean. If you were to take the dog right up to the curb edge, all that traffic would appear to the dog to be towering above him, which could cause your dog to be frightened. So take great care when you are getting your dog used to traffic. Once again, talk

While two members of the family enter the shop, the other two remain with their dog. In contrast, the owner of the dog tied up to the pole is nowhere to be seen.

to him, give him confidence and allow him to move around in the circular area around you on the full length of the leash.

Let Your Dog Rest

When you arrive home from a walk, allow your dog, especially if he is a puppy, to rest. His bed may be in the laundry, so put him in there and shut the door so that he is not disturbed. Like small children, it is most important that puppies get their sleep because they become mentally tired as well as physically tired.

If you have a kennel, use the same procedure. Ensure that it has clean, dry bedding with a suitable door on the kennel

This young dog has been carefully introduced to traffic and is now able to stand at the curb. The young handler strokes and talks to the dog reassuringly.

allowing plenty of fresh air in. It is not advisable to have the dog tied to the kennel by means of a chain. Dogs can become quite frustrated when tethered, which often leads to aggression. Once again, always make quite sure the dog has plenty of fresh drinking water.

Chapter 8
PLAYING WITH DOGS

There are several interesting games you can play with your dog. They are games that your dog will enjoy and that won't encourage unwanted habits. One of these games is retrieving. See if your dog will chase after a tennis ball, or even something a bit larger, and bring it back to you. If he does, praise him every time. Never chase after the dog, though. That will cause him to run off with the article and not come back to you.

Another game you can play with your dog is hide and seek. One person needs to hold the dog while another hides. When the person is hidden, the dog can be released; you will see him use his nose in trying to find the hidden person. When found, both people should praise the dog. In both these games, you can see that the dog is allowed and encouraged to come to you and find another person. These games will help you with your general dog training, which you should start very soon.

In addition to these games, make sure your puppy or dog has his own toys to play with and plenty of them too. Talk to your dog as he plays with his toys. Say something like this in a mysterious way, "What have you got then? Is that your toy? Oh! That's a neat toy, isn't it? Go on, run around with it. Good dog! Very good!" You can say the same things to your dog when you have

*These dogs thoroughly enjoy playing with their toys and will often bring them
to you as they greet your arrival home.*

him off the leash in a safe area and you see him pick up a stick.
Let your dog enjoy running around with it in his mouth. Some
dogs feel very proud just walking along with something to carry in
their mouths. Others will fling them out of their mouths and
chase after them again, and a few may even roll over on their
backs and play with pieces of sticks in their mouths, using their
front paws as if they were hands. All the time they are playing
these games, they just love to hear us talking to them and sharing
in their enjoyment. If you ever throw a stick for a dog, be very
careful. Sometimes, usually when the ground is soft, a stick can
land in the ground pointing slightly upwards. A stick stuck in the
ground at such an angle can be dangerous and can injure the
mouth of an enthusiastic dog as he grabs it. It is therefore safer if
you either hold the dog while you throw the stick sideways for it to
fall flat on the ground or throw a tennis ball instead.

Dogs and their owners enjoy playing together.

There is no need to make too many throws. A few each day is quite enough, especially for young dogs. Their limbs are growing and developing. Too much of this type of exercise can exhaust them.

There are, however, some games that are not advisable to play with your dog. Any wild type of game, like wrestling with the dog, even though he will enjoy it, will only excite him. Such games are highly likely to cause your dog to jump at you and others; mouth hands, ankles or garments; bark excessively; chase after you; run rings around you and generally act in a stupid way. Neither should you and your dog have a tug-o-war with something, nor should you chase after your dog around a tree or house furniture. By playing tug-o-war, you will be encouraging your dog to run off with things and not let you have them. By chasing your dog, you will destroy any hope of teaching him to come to you when called in the future. Dogs should never be teased in any way by people poking them or waving their hands around the dogs' heads. Such actions will cause dogs to start mouthing. This often leads to biting much harder in the future, and some dogs have become quite aggressive. Dogs can also become very disturbed at the sound of humans shouting and screaming. So every step should be taken to prevent dogs from being disturbed in these ways.

I always advise dog owners to have plenty of toys for their dogs. There is such a variety of toys for dogs on the market these days. You could buy a different toy from the pet shop every Christmas and also on your dog's birthdays. As he gets his new toy, put a name to it and use that particular name whenever he picks it up. One of my clients taught her German Shepherd Dog to get his toys by name. He thoroughly enjoyed the game. One day I visited her, and while he was playing with one toy in the sitting room where we were, she told him to fetch his new toy— a Teddy Bear. "Shane," she said, "go to your toy box and get your Teddy." He stood up and looked at her so much as to say, "Do I have to?" "Go on!" she urged him, "get your Teddy. The one you got for Christmas!" He trotted out to the laundry where his large toy box was situated. Then we heard much noise as he rummaged around to find his Teddy. Finally, there was silence and he came back into the sitting room proudly carrying his Teddy Bear. She then told him, "Take it over to Uncle Mike and show him!" This he did and quite willingly presented it to me. I said, "Give!" and as I took it from his mouth, I praised him as he released his grip on it. He was truly an amazing dog. She was always talking to him, and he virtually understood everything she said.

It is unfortunate that many dog owners, who try and do the best for their dogs, unwittingly play the wrong games with their dogs, like wrestling with them, playing tug-o-war or chasing them. Whenever I mention these games to people whose dogs I

By playing gentle games with your dog, you will encourage him to have good behavior at other times.

train, they are always ready to admit they have played such games, but can understand why they are wrong when it is explained to them. I quickly assure them that all is not lost; they can start again. We can all learn from our mistakes. I always find it amusing when I speak about this topic during a talk I may give to a large audience. I observe the expressions on people's faces and know which ones are guilty of playing the wrong games with their dogs. I then ask all those people if they have played such games with their dogs, and all admit that they have. They must think that I am a mind reader! But it is not very hard to detect when you watch their facial expressions.

Chapter 9
TRAVELING WITH YOUR DOG

Nearly everyone needs to take his or her dog by car to some place, and if the dog is not used to car travel, he is likely to be carsick or go quite crazy with excitement or stress, which is no pleasure for any owner or dog. So get your dog used to riding in the car at an early age. When you do this, try to make the trips short at first. If you have a puppy, always lift him into and out of a car. Never expect him to jump up into and out of a car. If you allowed this to happen, the puppy would put too much strain on his back legs in jumping up and too much strain on his front legs in jumping down. A puppy's bones and muscles are developing as he grows through puppyhood, and you must make sure that no strain is placed on those limbs. In the car, the best place for a puppy, or any dog, is in a secure traveling crate. If you must let your puppy out of his crate, you may want to place him on the floor in front of the front passenger seat, sitting between your legs. There he will not be thrown about. Although many people let their dog ride unrestrained in the backseat, this is a dangerous place for the dog. If your puppy is riding up front with you, you will also be able to keep him under control and calm by stroking him gently as you travel along.

Always carry a puppy into and out of a car.

Never leave your dog in a car with all the windows closed, especially on a hot day. Without adequate ventilation, dogs will bark and whine at first, then panic. A closed car can heat up rapidly within seconds, and many dogs have died in cars in such intense heat. Always carry a bottle of cold water and a bowl from which your dog can drink in the back of your car. It is surprising how thirsty dogs become, especially on long journeys.

When you do undertake a long journey in the car during hot, sunny days, if you happen to be going in one direction so that the sun is on one particular side of the car all the time, then put your dog on the shady side.

Before you venture on any journey, ensure that your dog has had a good opportunity to relieve himself before your departure. If it happens to be a long journey, then it will be necessary to stop periodically, get your dog out of the car on a leash and

Don't leave your dog in a car with the windows rolled up—cars get hot very quickly.

collar, take him to a waste piece of ground and tell him to "Get busy." Pick up after him with a plastic container and dispose of it appropriately as soon as you can.

To exercise some control over your dog, get him to sit while you open the car door, then tell him to jump inside on command and praise him as he obeys. Similarly, when you stop, tell him to stay while you open the car door, call him out on command and praise him as he responds. All this does not take long. It gives you a wonderful opportunity to exercise control over your dog. Dogs that jump out of cars as soon as you open the door show no respect for you. They are just showing that they want to have their own way.

It is not advisable to allow your dog to have his head out of the window when traveling. The wind and dust, also little flies, can get into your dog's eyes, which may result in the need for veterinary treatment.

For those people who by necessity have to convey their dogs in the backs of utility trucks, ensure that the dogs are securely fastened to the center so that they cannot jump over or fall over the sides of such vehicles.

If you ever happen to pull in to a gas station to fill up with gas, it is advisable to get your dog out of the car, make your approach toward the station attendant and even introduce your dog to the attendant, if he or she likes dogs.

Very often if a dog is left inside a car and the attendant makes a direct approach toward the near side window and inserts the gas nozzle into your car, making some noise in the process, the dog is likely to show some form of suspicion and start barking. This is because he suddenly sees the figure of a man approach the small window, which has a threatening effect. If the dog is taken out of the car and encouraged to approach the attendant, he feels so much more at ease.

You will often find that many dogs, when left in their cars while their owners are away for a certain length of time, while shopping, for instance, will get into the driver's seat, curl up and go fast off to sleep. Why do they do this? Well, naturally, when the owner has gone away, the dog feels a little bit lonely, so he goes to the seat that has a fair amount of the owner's body scent on it. It is, in fact, the next best thing to the owner from which the dog can seek any human comfort.

Laws about dogs accompanying owners on public transport and staying at hotels, motels and camping grounds can vary from state to state or country to country. It is best to check on all these regulations. But I have always believed that the best policy is to approach officials or proprietors and explain that you have a trained dog who is well behaved and ask if there would be any objection to you having him with you. In the vast majority of cases, I have been given a welcome response. In addition to this, I have also asked patrons if they have any objection to my having my dog with me. Once again, people welcome your request with a pleasant response. When they see that your dog is friendly and well behaved and that you care for him and handle him really well, they are only too happy to welcome you back in the future.

One most interesting thing about our dogs when they travel by car, and one which puzzles many people, is that regardless of the length of the journey, the various routes taken, whether it is day or night and whether the dog is fast asleep, the dog will wake within a few hundred yards of arriving home or at any destination to which your dog has traveled in the past.

How does the dog know? Well, it is all quite simple, really. Your home area or any area to where the dog is going has its own environmental smell. The dog recognizes the particular scent even though he is fast asleep. It indicates to him that the destination is very near, which results in him getting quite excited. Even if it is very dark outside and he cannot see anything, his sense of smell never fails him.

Even if all the windows of the car are closed, the scent of the area outside will enter through any small gaps in the car. You cannot keep that away from dogs. Aren't they fantastic animals?

Traveling on Buses and Trains

When traveling on buses and trains, a steady flow of passengers boards and alights at nearly every stop. It is safer for your dog if you allow him to stand in busy circumstances like these, because if you were to order him to sit or lie down, he might have his tail accidentally trodden on by one of the passengers. The same thing could apply on some long-distance trains, but usually there is a safe place for him to lie down, especially if you can obtain a window seat.

Traveling in trains, well-behaved dogs in compartments have often proved to be the center of attention and conversation among passengers.

Chapter 10
MANAGING BEHAVIOR PROBLEMS

Start With Praise

When you praise your dog, use praising words slowly and quietly in order to keep him calm. If you talk too quickly and/or loudly, you will probably excite him and he will jump around all over the place and probably jump up at you as well. At the same time, if you are in a stationary position, you can gently and very slowly stroke the dog on the head. This will keep your dog calm and attentive. But if you patted the dog, ruffled him up or stroked him quickly, you would then excite the dog and once again he could become boisterous, which would make controlling him difficult.

Jumping Up

Most friendly or excitable dogs will want to jump up at people. This can annoy, and in some cases frighten, many people. Therefore you must correct this unacceptable action or habit every time it happens. You will need to use a phrase like, "Get off!" or, "Get down!" Say it in a stern tone of voice as if you really mean it, then take hold of the clip end of the leash with one hand for a moment, jerk the dog down and let go of that part of the leash.

Always praise your dog gently and slowly to keep him calm and attentive.

As soon as the dog stands with all four feet on the ground, praise him slowly and quietly, "Good dog!" You have then praised him because he has obeyed you. Try not to say, "You bad dog!" How can he be a bad dog if he has obeyed? That doesn't make sense, does it? Lots of dogs get up to all kinds of mischief that is only

This lady is suddenly alarmed, throwing her hands up in the air, as the dog jumps up at her. The young lady quickly corrects her dog by saying, "Get off!" and jerks down on the leash. This is followed with praise as soon as her dog remains standing on the ground.

wrong in our eyes. What we have to do is to correct those faults and praise our dogs when they have obeyed and pleased us. As time goes on, our dogs should improve provided we train and handle them properly and kindly. So always believe you have a good dog, not a "bad dog."

Jumping at people entering your home is a habit many dogs develop. To avoid this, call out to the person on the other side, "One moment please, I'm just coming," before you open the door. Put your dog on a leash and collar and take him to the front door. Open it and welcome the visitors inside. If your dog jumps up at them, say, "No!" or, "Off!" and immediately jerk downwards on the leash. As soon as the dog stands on the ground, quietly and slowly praise him.

Then ask the visitors if they would mind stepping outside once more, close the door for a few seconds, open it and ask them in again. This time say to the dog in a warning tone of voice, "No! Off!" You will find that he will soon learn not to jump up when this has been repeated a few times. Don't forget to praise your dog when he has obeyed your warning.

Putting your dog on his leash before you open the door has another purpose. You are able to stop him from running out to the front of your property and possibly out to the road where he could get hurt or even killed. So remember, take all necessary precautions to prevent bad behavior and accidents.

Barking

I mentioned earlier that you should not allow your dog to bark at people in the street, although there will be times when you will want your dog to bark in order to warn you that someone is coming up the path to your house, or whenever there is a knock at your front door or the bell rings.

But when your dog has barked a few times, you will then need to tell him to stop by saying, "Quiet!" In quite a short time, your dog will know that while he is allowed to bark on those occasions, he must cease when you say, "Quiet!" Only use a word like "No!" when your dog is doing something that he is not allowed to do at all.

Your neighbors will be bothered by a dog who barks all the time.

Chewing

Dogs, and particularly puppies, often get up to all sorts of mischief. They love to explore bedrooms. If any clothes and shoes are left lying around, puppies are sure to find them and chew them into pieces. To prevent your dog from destroying your things, be sure to put everything away and shut the closet and bedroom doors.

If you have to go out for some time, do not let your dog have the run of the house. If you do, he is likely to chew furniture, carpets and curtains. It would, therefore, be safer to put him in a small room, like the laundry, where there is hardly anything for him to chew!

Correcting an Unleashed Dog

Earlier in this book, I explained how you should correct your dog when he pulls on the leash or jumps up at people: Give your dog a command and then immediately give him a jerk on the leash; as soon as he obeys, praise him. There will be times, of course, when you do not have the dog on the leash, so how are you going to correct the dog? Well, you should take hold of the dog by the scruff of his neck with both hands, one on each side of the dog's neck, say, "Get off!" and then give him a quick, firm up-and-down shake once or twice and let go immediately. If it is done properly, you will be surprised how well the correction works. As soon as the dog behaves, praise him quietly and slowly. The puppy or dog will know instinctively that that is a correction, because his own mother would have done that to any of her puppies when they misbehaved. When she corrected one of her puppies, she would use her mouth to pick him up by the scruff of his neck and give him a shake. The puppy would naturally let out a bit of a scream, but when she let go of him, he would show

The author shows how a corrective shake should be done. Taking hold of each side of the dog's neck with both hands, say, "Get off!" and give a quick, firm shake up and down, let go and praise quietly and slowly as soon as he has responded.

great respect for her by walking around her front feet and wagging his tail as if to say, "I'm awfully sorry, Mom, I won't do that again, really I won't!" The other good things about that correction are that the puppy neither becomes afraid of her nor challenges her authority again. So if we do the same by using our hands, we should get the same results that the mother dog got.

Small children should not be expected to do this, so their parents should do it themselves. Although it is easy to show people how to do this with a puppy or adult dog, many people wonder how quickly and firmly the correction should be done. Well, imagine someone is helping you fill a small sack of sand, and you want to get a bit more sand into the sack. Naturally, you would get a good grip with both hands on opposite sides of the rim of the sack and give it a couple of quick up-and-down shakes to make the level of the sand go down, wouldn't you? To do this you would have to have a good grip and a fair amount of strength, and you would need to act quickly. In much the same way, you will have to do that with a dog.

This type of correction is useful when your puppy or dog suddenly mouths you. When a dog mouths your hands, your ankles or even your clothes, he wants to have his own way. This must not be allowed. Remember, you are the boss. So give him that type of correction and say corrective words, such as "No!" or "Get off!" a fraction of a second before the actual shake. You may ask, "But the mother could not say those corrective words?" You are right. She couldn't. She gave a faint growl instead. Later, she would only have to give that growl and the puppies would respect her. Later, we will only have to say the words and our puppies and dogs will respect us. Isn't it interesting how they learn?

Punishment

Having explained all that, it is now very important for you to know what you must not do in correcting your dog, which is to never, never hit him for something that he has done wrong in your eyes. If you hit him and he is a timid dog by nature, he will become afraid of you and even run away and hide. But if he is a bold dog by nature, after he has had a few wacks (whether by using your hand, a rolled-up newspaper, a stick or anything else), he will turn aggressive and bite you.

There is a very true saying: "Never punish your dog, train him!" In my opinion, hitting a dog is a punishment. That is not the way to do it. Think for a moment, can or does the mother hit her puppies? No, she shakes them instead. So let us stick as close to nature as we possibly can and do as she does. So remember, never hit your dog.

The shake correction can be used at other times, such as when a puppy or dog chews the furniture, when he jumps up at you or other people or when you catch him in the act of digging holes or pulling the wash off the line. You can also use it for barking when he wants to come in and you want him to remain outside for a while, for stealing food off the table and for many other things.

Chapter 11
AS DOGS GET OLDER

We all have to put so much into bringing up our dogs in the first year of puppyhood. That is just the start. During the next few years, we should be giving our dogs further education by training them and taking them to a variety of places. If we do this, we can be proud of having well-behaved dogs who are also admired by other people outside of our own families.

It is generally accepted that one year in our lifetime is about the same as seven years in a dog's lifetime. Anyway, as the dog's lifetime rolls on, he becomes more mature and sensible, yet still very active. At around the age of 10 years, we begin to see most breeds gradually slow down. We see them not so keen to jump over things as they did when they were young, but instead they will choose to go around another way. Although they still like going for walks, they tend to tire more quickly; therefore, we should reduce the distance we used to walk them.

A number of dogs become deaf in their old age. Deafness can come on within a matter of a few weeks with some dogs. Likewise, many dogs' eyesight gradually fails until some become totally blind. This is when we all have to be very understanding and give them that extra loving care.

As dogs get older, they usually become less active. But they still enjoy spending time with their owners.

Perhaps the saddest thing about owning dogs is that they don't live as long as we would like them to live, but the greatest things that dogs give us are protection, enjoyment, loyalty, companionship and love.

In return, we should play our part in caring for the dog and providing for his needs. We should try to understand his feelings and how he sees us. We should give time to the dog and share in his happiness as he romps around us when we take him for walks. And we should be responsible in training him to be a well-behaved dog and liked by everyone he meets.

I've been training dogs for nearly half a century. It has been a wonderful life for me. I never tire from training—I love it too much. The rewards have been most varied and great, and I always like dog owners to get just as much enjoyment as I do in caring for, living with and training their dogs.

It is always a joy for me to meet up again with people and dogs I trained many years ago. And when I see how well behaved those dogs are, now that they are getting older, I, like their owners, can look back and say how worthwhile it has all been to train them to be so well accepted into the community.

Through five decades, I have seen how dog training in many fields has progressed. Trainers and instructors all over the world have strived to improve the training and have had visions of the future and of using dogs for so many good causes. One of these is the Pets As Therapy program (P.A.T.) in several countries in the world. Dogs with friendly temperaments who are basically obedient have been placed in nursing homes, rehabilitation centers and other places where they have brought much happiness to those who are bedridden, in wheelchairs, lonely and unable to move around as they did years ago.

Because there are not enough of these P.A.T. dogs to be permanently placed in these homes, an increased number of volunteers with their own pet dogs are supporting this program. Quite a number of these dogs are getting older now, but they are doing a fantastic job visiting, not only nursing homes and rehabilitation centers, but hospitals, too. I have been personally involved in this work for the last 10 years and have seen the great work our dogs have done during their scheduled visits.

Not all of these dogs have been owned since they were small puppies. Many of them were acquired when they were a year or more old. I always make a point of asking the owners a little bit of their dog's history when assessing their temperament and behavior for the P.A.T. program as we walk through a shopping center. These dogs must be quite sound with the sight and noise of traffic, shopping carts coming toward them and a multitude of other things seen in the streets. But in particular, we need to see how friendly each dog is when he is handled by perfect strangers—men, women and children of all ages. To give a few examples of the dogs' previous homes, a number of them were abandoned because their original owners had no more time for them. Others were left in their backyards all day. Because they were bored, they barked and howled. This annoyed the neighbors, who made official complaints. Finally, the owners were advised that unless the dog was found a suitable home, he would have to be destroyed. A few, it was alleged, were sheep worriers. They likewise came under the same threat. Some, however, were cared for very well by their breeders, but because they were not successful in the show world, they were sold off as the breeders had no more use for them. Yet all these dogs were at last given the opportunity to do this fantastic work in the P.A.T. program. Added to this, many of these dogs, who have been virtually rescued by their present owners, have been trained in obedience, and some have been awarded obedience titles. Many rewarding stories could be told about these dogs, I am sure.

Directors of nursing have told us how the patients so look forward to the weekly visits made by a variety of our dogs, how they enjoy their company on the day and how they talk about visits for days later.

The dogs have also had a calming influence on many of the patients' visitors, who for numerous reasons are under some strain and stress. And it hasn't stopped there. The dogs have had a great effect on the nursing and medical staff in these establishments, for they too are under great strain at times. To see a lovely, happy dog walk into a ward or private room is like a breath of fresh air and creates a new topic of conversation. Medical research has found that the presence of a dog has helped to even reduce high blood pressure in a number of people. Some patients, after meeting these dogs, have started talking again, whereas in the past, other methods have failed.

These are just a few examples; others are too numerous to record here.

So here is work that dogs of all ages can do, but particularly older dogs who are very content with this more relaxed way of life. Years ago, who would have dreamed of dogs being trained for this work?

PART 2
Obedience Training

Chapter 12
THE BASICS

Basic obedience training is the foundation for all types of dog training. For example, gun dogs, sheep dogs, police dogs, guide dogs and many other working dogs must first undergo basic training. Training is based on the respect and affection the dog has for his owner. Affection from the dog is not hard to achieve. You only have to love your dog, feed him, groom him, take him out for walks and share his company and your dog will return all your love by showing his affection for you. Although it is easy to gain your dog's affection, it is harder to gain his respect so that he obeys you implicitly.

You have to make the obedience exercises as easy as possible for the dog to understand. You have to show him exactly what you want him to do. You have to concentrate one hundred percent on the dog, use the correct words of command, use your hands and the dog's leash correctly and, above all, be consistent with everything you do if you are to achieve success.

Be patient and firm, but never allow yourself to lose your temper nor give into the dog if he tries to have his own way.

Never train a dog for too long. Dogs cannot concentrate for long periods of time, as they soon become tired. Whatever you

*Try to train your dog when the weather is nice. Neither of you
want to be outside on a cold, rainy day.*

teach your dog, do it in a simple way with accuracy and make the
training enjoyable with plenty of praise.

Pick a good time of the day to train your dog; train when the weather is cool, dry and mild. Do not train in strong winds—they disturb even the best of trained dogs. Select a good place: In the early days, pick a fairly quiet place with only a few distractions around, not a busy, noisy area. Later, vary the training ground and visit different places.

Another old theory, which is sometimes suggested today, is to train a dog to do an exercise perfectly before going on to another exercise. If you were to follow that theory, it would take years to train your dog to do all the basic exercises. Besides that, your dog would become bored stiff with having to do the same exercise day after day.

The best theory to follow is to train your dog to do an exercise like heel and sit in a straight line, and as long as he has a fairly good idea of what it is all about, then teach the three turns in the next lesson. As time goes on, you will achieve perfection with all the exercises and your dog will enjoy the variety of exercises you are teaching him daily. When you have perfected each exercise, it is not necessary to get the dog to do every exercise every day. With some exercises, you only need to practice them once or perhaps twice a week at the most.

Make sure that you have good training equipment. You will need a suitable, strong slip-chain collar and a strong leash of correct length. The leash should be comfortable in your hands.

Stick strictly to the basic principles of training. If you do not, or you find that you are not being consistent, your dog will become confused and either perform incorrectly or not at all. Think very carefully about what you are going to do at all times. Never worry if something goes wrong or your dog does not do the exercise very well, just calmly do it again. Remember the old proverb, "Rome wasn't built in a day!"

Chapter 13
GETTING STARTED

I have always believed that when a puppy or adult dog comes into a family home, everyone should share in his welfare and upbringing.

Naturally, I would never expect very young children to control dogs. That should be done by parents, particularly when the puppy or dog needs to be corrected. With parental guidance, older children, provided they have the capabilities, can learn how to train their pets. Older children should be supervised when they train and walk their dogs.

I wish to emphasize here that when you train your dog or walk him on a slip-chain collar, he should be handled correctly and with great care. How to use a slip-chain collar and leash is explained later in this book.[1]

While much can be learned from books, dog training is a skill to be learned practically. Voice control can only really be taught and mastered in practical lessons. The correct intonation of voice has to be practiced repeatedly. It is not so much what you say to the dog, as how you say it that counts. The printed word, in this respect, is not as effective as the spoken word.

Training Classes

You can learn dog training by either joining an obedience dog training club or receiving individual attention from a professional dog trainer on a one-to-one basis.

Start by consulting the Yellow Pages, which lists dog training clubs and trainers in your area. Arrange to visit classes to observe and listen to the way both owners and dogs are instructed, the methods used, the class sizes and the general standards of work. You may also want to call the American Kennel Club, or the Association of Pet Dog Trainers, accredited professional dog trainers and veterinarians. These people will be happy to advise you where and where not to go. It is a great help if you happen to know someone who has trained at a particular dog school that can be highly recommended.

I would not recommend any dog training group that trains entirely with a food incentive. Often dog owners are asked not to feed their puppies for at least 12 hours prior to an instructional lesson. This request can be for longer periods, anything up to 48 hours if the dog is older. No puppy or adult dog should ever be starved for this purpose. Naturally, when a dog is so hungry, he will do anything for a tidbit of food. But when he is not hungry, chances are he won't obey. Therefore, it is a very unreliable way of training—nothing more than a bribe, in my opinion. Good training is based on respect and affection the dog shows toward his handler.

Selecting a Training Class

Before you sign up, be quite sure that you feel comfortable with what you see. If you can, speak to some of the instructors after they have finished training a class. They can usually answer most of your queries, but please don't burden them with all your problems!

There are certain dog training schools I would not recommend, namely those that teach any form of "attack work" for protection purposes. You don't need a dog trained to attack. It can be a very dangerous practice. This type of training should only be carried out in police dog schools and the armed services.

Also, consider finances. Generally, it is less expensive to join an obedience dog club, but with large classes, it is hard to get any individual attention. The instructors, who are volunteers, will probably have neither the time nor the expertise to deal with problem dogs. In such cases, they should, and often will, refer an owner to a professional trainer for individual classes.

Naturally, a professional trainer charges more than a volunteer. And provided he or she is an accredited trainer with much experience, both owner and dog can be diagnosed and corrected in a very short time. Many clients have stated that they achieved far better results during a few private lessons than attending an obedience dog club for many months and having very little to show for their efforts. For them, private lessons worked out to be more cost effective.

Care should be taken when seeking the services of people who call themselves professional dog trainers or instructors. In recent years, many unqualified individuals have jumped on the bandwagon, often charging exorbitant fees. They often use much technical jargon to impress clients. A good instructor will use simple language, especially when instructing children, and show how good results can be gained quite easily in a short span of time.

Check out the instructor's credentials and past experience. Just because a person has trained a few dogs who have been very successful in obedience trials, does not mean that the person has a great ability to instruct people, nor does it show that he or she has vast experience training a wide range of breeds. So shop around; if you are not happy with the way the instructor conducts the training for you, your child and your dog, then look elsewhere.

I would not expect a child to train a dog until he or she is about 10 years of age. Even then it would depend largely on the child's attitude toward, and interest in, training. Other factors would also have to be taken into consideration: the child's reflexes, learning ability, use of voice, powers of concentration, physical build and strength as opposed to the dog's size, weight, strength, responsiveness and other temperamental characteristics.

Generally, girls seem to do better than boys at dog training. One of the reasons for this is that girls mature earlier. It is noteworthy that those who have had experience horseback riding are very good dog trainers. These children have already developed a good rapport with an animal. Boys don't take up horseback riding as frequently as girls do, but the boys who are very good at dog training are often excellent at mathematics and science. These subjects require an ability to work out problems with a logical step-by-step approach, an ability that is reflected in dog training. Interesting, isn't it?

Very young children have an important role to play within the family who owns a dog. I always welcome it when parents bring their dog to me for training and are accompanied by one or more young children.

I always take the opportunity to show young children how to talk quietly and kindly to their dogs, and how to stroke them gently and slowly in order to keep the dogs calm and make them feel loved. I also advise children never to scream at or tease their dogs, because this will cause the dogs to become very upset. And, most important, children must be taught to never hit their dogs. A dog who has been struck may bite the child in anger.

Some children take to dog training naturally. It is always a good idea to walk the dog freely, as above, for a few minutes before you start the heelwork.

When very young children are brought up to learn to love and handle dogs kindly, they are taking an important step. As they grow up, they will be better able to care for and handle their dogs and to develop a wonderful relationship with them.

[1]*Further information can be obtained by reading my books:* Dog Training Made Easy *and* Solving Your Dog Problems *(Published by Howell Book House, New York, NY).*

Chapter 14
WALKING COMMANDS

Walking at Heel

The first exercise that you should teach your dog is to walk at heel on your left side on a slack leash. Using your right hand, hold the leash handle first, plus one other point down the leash, so that the rest of the leash between your right hand and the dog hangs down in a "U" shape. Never have it tight. Say the dog's name, say "Heel!" and then step forward. Your dog will see you go and, wanting to go with you, will move one of his front paws forward. As soon as you see your dog's front paw move forward, praise him by saying, "Good dog!" so that he understands that he has done the right thing at the right time at the right place.

While your dog walks next to you with his head beside your left knee, everything is all right. Sooner or later, however, most dogs will go too far forward and need to be corrected immediately. Take hold of the clip end of the leash in your left hand, say in a firm voice, "Heel!" and give the dog a quick, horizontal jerk backwards along the surface of his back. Then let go and stand perfectly still. Wait for a few seconds, then, provided your dog has remained quite still beside you, start again by saying, "Laddie, heel!" and step forward; he will follow and you will praise him.

Before you heel your dog forward, ensure you are holding the leash correctly in the right hand; keep your left hand off of it. Holding on with your left hand will cause tension on the leash, which will make your dog pull.

Walking a dog perfectly at heel, the handler has to keep his eyes on his dog, keep the leash slack, talk quietly and look where he is going.

Repeat the correction every time the dog goes too far forward. Remember to *always* stop when this happens. This makes the dog realize that he has to be at your side. If you jerk the dog back without stopping, you will find that he will put up with all the jerks and keep leading out in front of you because you are still moving. But if you stop each time, that is quite different. He will realize that he *has* to stop and that he is not allowed to go forward again until he is invited by you to do so.

98

*To correct the dog when he goes too far ahead, take hold of the clip part of the leash in the left hand, say "Heel!" firmly, give a backward jerk, let go and **stand perfectly still.***

Sit

When you want to make your dog sit, prepare for it while you are still walking along by putting the clip part of the leash into your right hand, holding it directly above your dog's head. Now place your left hand over his hindquarters with your thumb pointing to the left, as if you were going to throw a ball underhand. Say the word "Sit!" quickly and sharply, but not loudly. Push the dog's hindquarters downward and slightly forward as you keep your right hand in a set position vertically above his head. As soon as the dog sits, praise him quietly and gently and let go of

99

When you make your dog sit, make it easy on yourself and the dog by doing it accurately so that the dog learns the right way by habit.

the clip part of the leash so there is no more tightness on his neck.

Often a dog may sit in a floppy position, such as with his right hind leg tucked under him and protruding to his left. When this occurs, the dog should be corrected by simply

Always praise the dog quietly and gently in order to keep him calm and attentive.

Always remember to dismiss your dog from a short training lesson so that he can walk along again and relax.

running the back of your left hand down the right-hand side of his body and very gently lifting his right leg out so that he sits up straight. Then praise him. In time he will find out that you will not allow him to sit in a lazy position and that he will not receive praise until he sits properly.

Walking your dog at heel along a straight path for about 80 yards with five or six "Sit" commands should take about five minutes. That is long enough. When you have praised your dog at the last "Sit," you will need to dismiss him, just as a school-teacher dismisses a class of children so that they can go out onto the playground. Show your dog that the training lesson has now finished by saying something like, "Go free!" or, "Off you go and play!" At the same time, give a signal from under his chin by spreading both of your hands forward and outward down the path. That will show the dog what you are allowing him to do— walk free. After about five to ten minutes of free walking, you could do another five minutes of heelwork. Don't forget the dismissal at the end of each short lesson; otherwise, he will never understand when the lesson is finished. It is very much like when we were all at school and the teacher dismissed the class at the end of the lesson; we all knew that we could then go out onto the playground until we were all called in for the next lesson. Such work and dismissals continue with many things we do in our lives. It is like being on-duty and off-duty, and the same applies when training and working with dogs.

Right-About Turn

When you have taught your dog to walk at heel and sit reasonably well in a long straight line, you can teach him the right-about turn. As you walk along, put all of your leash in the left hand. Put both of your hands down to the dog's eye level and pat your right leg with your right hand a few times as you say your dog's name and "Heel!" in an interesting tone of voice. The noise you make slapping your right leg should attract the dog to follow you around to the right as you pick up your feet on the spot. As soon as you have turned around, continue walking up the path you came down. Praise the dog as he turns with you, and keep the leash *slack*. It might be necessary to give the dog a jerk with the left hand if he does not obey immediately. When you have done the turn, put the leash back into the right hand. Do two of these turns about eight yards apart, continue walking for a while and do two more. This turn is very good for getting your dog to watch with interest which way you are going, and it is good for getting your dog to give you more respect.

*The right-about turn: To capture the dog's attention, use a most interesting tone of voice as you say the dog's name and "Heel!" and pat your right leg with your right hand a few times. Praise the dog as he turns his head around, and keep the leash **slack**.*

Right Turn

You will find this very easy after you have taught your dog the right-about turn, because it is only half the angle, namely, 90 degrees. You may like to try it in a park or on a marked tennis court by heeling your dog around a square or rectangle. The white lines on a tennis court help to keep you walking straight. Just do four turns. That's enough. Too many turns will bore your

Having walked along the footpath, this young handler has decided to do a right turn to the curb and then cross over the road.

dog. Don't forget to get your dog's attention *before* you turn your feet in the next direction.

Left Turn

This turn is even easier than the right turn because you don't have to keep moving the leash from one hand to the other and back again. Carry the leash in the right hand all the time. To turn left, take hold of the clip part of the leash with your left hand for one moment, say "Heel!" very quickly and give a short jerk along the surface of the dog's back. The dog will suddenly stop; in that moment, spin on the ball of your left foot and your right foot will come around automatically, taking the next step across the front of the dog. This shows the dog which way he has to go. And that is all there is to it. You could practice this turn in

Having crossed the street, the handler has decided to turn left along the sidewalk.

a square too, going around in the opposite direction. Four turns are quite enough. If you went around in squares all the time, your dog would become bored very soon. Now that you know how to go forward, do the three different turns and sit the dog, make it more natural for your dog by including the different turns in a short walk.

Walk your dog at heel along a path or sidewalk, do a left turn to the curb and get him to sit at the curb's edge. When there is no traffic approaching, cross the street, turn right on the path and, after walking a little way, turn right to the curb and sit. When safe, cross the street again and turn left on the sidewalk. Somewhere along that stretch of sidewalk you could do two right-about turns. By training your dog this way, he feels as if he is going somewhere and you are putting in the different turns, the curb sits and road crossings as you go. Never let your dog

sniff the ground when heeling. If he does, say "Leave!" and jerk
the leash up with your left hand. As soon as his nose comes away
from the ground, praise him. Remember that your dog must pay
attention to you when he is heeling. If he is allowed to sniff
around, he won't be taking any notice of you.

Two sessions of five minutes of training with a break between
the sessions is quite enough for a young dog when he first starts
training. The rest of the exercise should be free walking so that he
can relax and be introduced to all sorts of exciting things.

Earlier, I said that the left turn is easier than the right, yet
there are a few people who find it hard to perform. It is generally because they find it hard to coordinate their vocal command
with their left-hand jerk, and this horizontal backward hand jerk
with the spin on the ball of their left foot.

I have found that the vast majority of the people who have
this coordination difficulty have never taken up sports of any
kind, nor have they done any handicrafts. Those who have
participated in sports or dance, or who have served in the armed
services, police force, fire service or a number of other occupa-
tions, have no difficulty with coordination.

So to help those who have difficulty, I ask them to watch me
walk around in a small square without a dog, doing nothing but
left turns without stopping. Then I ask them to do the same
while I hold their dog. When they have mastered their footwork,
I ask them to go around again, giving an imaginary backward
jerk on the leash just as their left foot is about to come down on
the ground. When they can do these two things, I ask them to go
around again and give the one quick word, "Heel!" before they
give the horizontal backward jerk with their left hand. When
they have mastered all three things—the voice, the jerk and the
spin on the ball of the left foot—I hand their dog back and ask
them to do it this time with the dog. The results are always most

pleasing. It is amazing what can be achieved if the correct and simple technique is shown.

A most interesting observation I have made in recent years concerns the left turn. Having trained thousands of men, women and children with their dogs, I have found that when I taught the adults to do the left turn, they would always jerk the dog away to the left of them instead of giving a little jerk horizontally backward to stop the dog for a fraction of a second. But whenever I trained children, they had no trouble and did it with precision. Why was this? Before I go on to explain what I found out, I can just imagine the children who are reading this saying to themselves, "Well, that is something we, as children, can do better than adults!" I certainly cannot criticize you for thinking in that way. Anyway, it baffled me for years, until one day when a middle-aged lady came to me for training with her crossbred dog. She had never trained a dog before.

During the second lesson, I taught her the left turn and was amazed how she did it with precision the first time. Her husband did not walk along with us, but sat in his car reading the newspaper! At the end of the lesson, she made an appointment to see me the following week and got into the car to go home. It was then that I learned that she had never driven a car in her life. She had never wanted to learn to drive. She relied on her husband to drive her wherever she wanted to go. At this point, a flash went through my mind: She had never driven a car, but she had just performed a left turn for the first time with absolute precision. Surely, there must be some connection, I thought. What had she in common with all the children I had trained? It was, of course, that none of them had ever driven a car. All the other adults who had come to my school for dog training were licensed to drive cars. When I taught them the left turn, they automatically thought that they were turning the steering wheel to the left; in consequence, they jerked the leash in the same direction. It was gratifying to me to discover the reason for this action, which had puzzled me for years. You never stop learning, do you?

You may well ask by this time why it is important for you to learn how to teach your dog these simple turns and for him to do them.

First, when you teach these three turns, you will get even more attention from your dog, and he will show you even more respect. His whole future relationship with you depends on this respect. Training is based on the affection and respect you have for each other. You also have to be very consistent in everything you do with your dog if you wish to achieve and maintain success.

Often, clients will comment, after a few lessons, that they have noticed that their dog has become better behaved at home and also in other places where they happen to take him. They ask if it is coincidence, or if the obedience training out on the streets had anything to do with his improved behavior at home and other places. It is certainly not coincidence but definitely the training that has calmed the dog down and taught him to respect the home and those who live in it.

Second, learning how to do these turns teaches a handler a tremendous amount. It teaches you to keep your eyes on your dog and watch every response he makes. You learn how to use your voice and the right intonation you have to make with every word depending on the situation. You learn how to hold the leash correctly depending on the exercise you are teaching your dog. You learn how to use your hands in praising, encouraging and correcting the dog. You learn how to coordinate everything and get your timing right. You gradually develop the art of anticipating your dog's behavior, and you learn to watch out for the unexpected to happen, like a cat running across the road, which might excite the dog and cause him to chase the cat.

All this basic training and more prepares you for the time when you train your dog to do something far more demanding, like commanding him to come when he is playing with several other dogs. Yes, I can hear you saying, "That's asking a lot from a dog!" Yes, it is, but the only way you will achieve that goal is to first lay a solid foundation of basic training.

Occasionally, I do have some people who cannot see the importance of doing all these turns and sits. All they want is to have their particular problems ironed out. Most of those problems exist because their dogs have no respect for their owners whatsoever. I just tell them that there are no magic wands in dog training. Owners must face up to their responsibilities and learn how to train their dogs. In fact, they have far more to learn than their dogs.

Chapter 15
THE COME COMMAND

The most important exercise to teach any dog is the come command—where the dog is taught to come when he is least expecting it.

You never know when you might have to call your dog in an emergency. For example, you would need to call your dog if he was running away from you toward a busy road or toward anything dangerous, or if he was running after or making a nuisance of himself with people or other animals. And of course, you will need to call your dog in order to put him on his leash to return home and in many other situations.

It is not as hard as you first might think to teach this exercise; in fact, it is quite easy. Let's imagine that your dog's name is Rex and you are walking him along a sidewalk on the *full* length of the leash and he is just out in front of you. Suddenly, say in a most enthusiastic voice, "Rex, come!" and step backwards. As he turns to come to the front of your body, praise him. When you have stepped backwards three or four steps, take up half the length of the leash in one hand (so that he doesn't get his legs tangled in the leash), and keep both of your hands as if handcuffed together between your knees. This will help attract him to the center of your body. Walk backwards slowly to keep him

Call the dog enthusiastically, using his name and "Come!" and walk backwards. Praise the dog the moment he turns around toward you.

As the dog comes toward you, take up half the length of the leash and keep both hands together between your knees to attract him straight toward you.

calm, and talk to him nicely so that he is pleased to come. If he does get distracted, make use of your other hand by taking hold of the clip end of the leash. Say "Come," jerk him across to the front of you at his height and praise him by saying, "Good dog!" He will soon learn that if he goes to either side of you, he will be corrected, but if he comes straight to you, he will be praised. When he has done fairly well, gather all the leash into one hand (right down to the clip) and, with your other hand poised above his hindquarters, say "Sit!" Hold the leash up toward your

As the dog comes right up to you, have your hands prepared to sit him straight.

When praising, allow your dog to rest his lower jaw in the fingers of both hands while you praise quietly and slowly. Continue to keep his attention until you dismiss him.

stomach as you push and guide his hindquarters down and toward you. Praise him immediately, and when you do this, hold the clip part of the leash in one of your hands (let the rest of the leash drop on the ground if you like) and allow the dog to rest his lower jaw in the fingers of both your hands, while you very slowly stroke him with your thumbs only from his eyebrows to his ears. As you do this, keep saying quietly, "There's a good dog, very good! What a clever boy you are. Good dog!" The fingertips of your right hand should just be touching or nearly touching those of your left hand.

Keep Your Dog's Attention

While you are praising your dog for coming to you, make sure that he does not look around at people, dogs, cats or other distractions. If he does look around while you are praising him, he will think that you are praising him for looking at all those distractions, and that would never do, would it? If he does look around, stop praising him for a moment and correct him by either giving him an upward jerk on the leash or by giving him a quick little shake on the neck with both hands. I'm sure you know how to do that by now. And as soon as he looks at you, you know what to say. Yes, that's right: "Good dog!" Finally, dismiss your dog by telling him to "Go free! Go and play!" When he does, he can look at anything he wants to.

Do you see now how all the training is coming together like a jigsaw puzzle? Interesting, isn't it? And as you go on, you will find it more and more interesting and should get a great kick out of it.

A sidewalk is a very good place to practice the recall. It helps to keep you straight as you walk backwards down the center, and very often there are lots of nice smells on each side that your dog would like to sniff. So this gives you the chance to teach him to come to you and to correct him if he is distracted by juicy smells or anything else.

After about a week, by which time your dog should know what the recall is all about, try calling him in a *safe* place, like the rear of your property. As you walk along, drop the leash out of your hand, step backwards and call your dog. Praise him as soon as he turns around to come to you. Pretend that you are still holding the leash by using your hands in gathering an invisible leash! Just as your dog reaches you, take hold of the clip end of the leash, put your other hand over his hindquarters, say "Sit!" quickly and push and guide his hindquarters down and toward

113

Having dropped the leash out of your hand, walk backward and call your dog. Pretend you are gathering an invisible leash. This nearly always makes the dog think that he is still on the leash.

you. Praise him before he has the chance to look around at anything. Finally, dismiss your dog while he is looking at you and only you.

When Your Dog Doesn't Come

You may ask what you should do if, having dropped the leash, your dog doesn't come to you when called. That is simple. Walk forward, take hold of the handle of the leash, say "Come!" and give it a horizontal jerk toward you. Praise your dog immediately even though you have made him obey. You have to show him that you are the boss, but you are also a loving boss. Proper training of your dog means that you never get annoyed with him.

With time, you should improve as a trainer. If, however, you do have difficulties, start from the beginning again. It won't take long, and it is the best way to overcome faults.

Chapter 16
COMMANDS TO KEEP YOUR DOG STILL

The Sit-Stay Command

The sit-stay command is an important exercise because you will need to use it in many different situations. For example, you will need it whenever and wherever you need to leave your dog for a short period of time while you do something or prepare for the next part of an exercise, like a recall from a sit-stay position, or while you position yourself to call him over a jump (which I shall talk about later).

You have already taught your dog to sit; now he has to learn to stay put while you leave him and walk around in front to face him.

Make sure that he is sitting comfortably and note exactly the piece of ground on which he is sitting and the direction you have made him face. Hold your leash in the left hand vertically above his head, say "Stay!" and turn around to face your dog, so that you are one straight arm's length away—no farther. If he moves to get up, quickly say "Sit!" and give a quick little jerk upward on the leash, then relax the leash again. This should work if you are very quick in your correction. If the dog moves completely off the spot of ground where you had told him to

Sit-stay: Command "Stay!" and then step slowly around to face your dog at one straight arm's length away.

Holding the leash vertically above the dog's head, you are in the ideal position to correct the dog if he moves.

stay, then you must take him back to it again, make sure he faces in the same direction as before and repeat the exercise.

When the dog has stayed still for a few seconds, return to his right side, wait for a few more seconds, praise him and then dismiss him. It is very important that you wait for a few more seconds before you praise your dog. If you praised him the moment you returned to his side, he would soon begin to antici-pate this, and because he likes being praised, he is likely to get up and come toward you before you get back to his side. So by standing beside your dog for a short time, you will keep him guessing as to when you are going to praise him. Do not always

*In this next stage, you can be farther away from
your dog with the leash on a large loop.*

*If the dog attempts to move, step forward, taking hold near
the clip of the leash with the other hand, say "Sit!" and jerk
the leash up above the dog's head. Then let go, say "Stay"
and step backward again.*

dismiss your dog after the praise, sometimes say "Heel!" and walk
a bit farther, stop, praise and dismiss him. Once again, you can
see how you can keep the dog guessing as to what you are going
to do next. This also keeps him alert.

As the weeks go by and your dog becomes more obedient in
the sit-stay, you can lengthen the leash, which will then allow you
to get a bit farther away from the dog. Move slowly around in a
semi-circle in front of the dog. Step sideways when you do this
and watch him all the time. If he should get up, step forward
quickly and, by taking hold of the leash a few inches away from

the clip with your other hand, say "Sit!" and jerk the leash up above his head. Then let go, say "Stay" and step backwards again. Always stay in the semi-circle in front of the dog, so that he can see you walk around in front of him. If you walk around the back of your dog, he is sure to turn his head around and get up. I'm sure you will agree that if you did that in his early days of training, it would be expecting too much of the dog, which would be unfair, wouldn't it? For a few weeks, get the dog to really understand the exercise. When he has, you will find that he won't mind at all when you go around the back of him and stand beside him.

The Stand Command

The stand is a useful exercise and quite easy to teach. There will be times when you are walking your dog at heel and have to stop at the roadside. It may be raining, and the ground may be very muddy. Well, you certainly wouldn't want to sit your dog in puddles and mud, would you? So this is where the stand command can be used. It can also be used when you want to groom or bathe your dog and when the vet wants to examine him on the table. It is also possible that one day you might like to enter your dog in a dog show or an obedience trial in which your dog is required to stand.

Bring your dog to heel, but don't sit him, just let him stand there. Now imagine that you are walking your dog at heel and you want him to suddenly stand still. Put the clip part of the leash into your right hand and put your left hand over the dog's body. Place it just in front of the dog's left hind leg. That is called his stifle. Imagine that you are still walking along. Now give the command "Stand!" and then immediately give a quick little jerk back (just as you did in the left turn). At the same time, lock the left hind leg back a little with your left hand so there is little chance of the dog going into the sit position. Now let go of the clip part of the leash and bring your left hand forward to stroke the side of the dog's face gently and slowly. Now, would you like to practice that again while you are standing there? Just imagine that you are walking along in a straight line. That's good. Quite easy, isn't it?

Now that you know what to say and how to use your hands, try about four stand commands as you walk in a straight line. Give a stand command about every 10 yards. Don't add any sits or turns to the work, just simple heeling and standing.

Having done that, I think you can all give yourselves a pat on the back. The main reason why you found that exercise quite easy was that you have gained much experience in the past few weeks. You know what you are doing and are becoming more and more confident. And so is your dog.

Did you notice how you went about teaching your dog to stand? You went about it in much the same way that you taught him to sit weeks ago. First, you thought about it, didn't you? You made up your mind that you were going to get your dog to stand. Second, you made sure that your dog was paying attention. Third, you prepared everything; you put the clip part of the leash into your right hand and put your left hand over the dog's body, just in front of his left hind leg. Fourth, you gave the command "Stand!" Fifth, you used both of your hands at exactly the same time; you gave a little horizontal backward jerk on the leash and your left hand touched the front edge of the dog's left hind leg. Sixth, your dog obeyed, didn't he? Finally, you praised your dog for doing the exercise. So seven things actually happened. Isn't that interesting? Try and remember those seven points in that order, because you will need to use them whenever you teach something new to your dog.

Stand: Command "Stand!" and jerk horizontally backward on a short leash.
Lock the dog's left hind leg back a bit with your left hand.

The Down or Drop Command

The main reason why we teach a dog to lie down is that when we want the dog to stay for a long time, it would be considered unkind for him to stay in the sitting position. In the down position, a dog can relax more and even sleep a little if tired.

There are several ways to put a dog into the down position, so it is a good idea to use the method that suits your dog best.

Sit your dog beside you. You now have his hindquarters down on the ground. Now it is just a case of getting the front of the dog down. So try tapping the ground directly beneath his chin with your right hand. Dogs who are particularly inquisitive will often go down immediately to see what you are doing. Some-

The First Principles of Training

1. Make your **DECISION**

2. Have your dog's **ATTENTION**

3. **PREPARE** for the exercise

4. Give the **COMMAND**

5. Carry out your **ACTION**

6. Your dog **RESPONDS**

7. **PRAISE** your dog

An easy way to remember those seven points is to take the first letter of each of those key words; you will see that together they spell DAPCARP. With time, you will not have to make actions with your hands, your dog will just obey your commands. I can hear you say, "That will be great when we get to that stage." Yes, it will, and it won't be long before you achieve that stage if you continue to train well.

times a little extra help is needed with your left hand on the dog's shoulders to guide him down. However, if and when it happens, praise your dog by saying, "Good dog!" and slowly stroke him from under his chin toward his chest. Your dog should like that so much that he will want to stay there. If you stroked the dog on top of his head, he would like that, too, and would probably rise up for more, which you don't want to happen.

If that method does not work, don't worry. Try this instead: Place your left hand on your dog's shoulders. Turn yourself to face the dog's side. Kneel down on your right knee. Pass your right arm behind your dog's right knee and take hold of his left knee. Say "Down!" Gently lift both of his legs up and guide him down with your left hand, which is on his shoulder blades. As soon as the dog lies down, stroke him under the chin with your right hand. It is best for you to keep your left hand on the dog's shoulders. If he tries to get up, just push him gently down. After several seconds, dismiss your dog. As the days go by, you can get your dog to stay for longer periods of time.

The best time to start this exercise is either at the end of an obedience lesson or sometime in the evening when the dog is a bit tired. Don't attempt to teach it when he is highly excited at the beginning of the day or at the start of an obedience lesson. If you do, he will probably resist and give you a lot of trouble.

Always teach this command on comfortable ground, which means on soft grass outside or on a carpet indoors. Never start teaching it on rough, stony ground, or highly polished surfaces inside where the dog may slide and then panic. This applies to other exercises as well, but particularly the down.

The Stand-Stay & the Down-Stay Commands

When you have taught your dog to stand and lie down, you can teach him to stay in those positions just as you taught him to stay in the sit position. Remember to say "Stay!" only once and turn around to face your dog, then move from side to side, keeping your leash slack and your eyes always on your dog.

Recall from Sit-Stay Position

When you have taught your dog to come and to sit-stay, you can put the two together.

Down: With your left hand on the dog's shoulders, say "Down!" and gently lift both of his front legs and guide him down.

As soon as the dog lies down, praise him quietly and stroke him slowly under his chin toward his chest. Keep your left hand on the dog's shoulders.

Stand-stay: It helps if you do this exercise with the dog's front paws on a step. The dog is not so likely to move forward.

Down-stay: Keeping the leash slack in one hand, it often helps to raise the index finger of your other hand near your face to keep the dog's attention on you.

When to Use Your Dog's Name in Training

Have you noticed that when we train our dogs, sometimes we use their names before the actual commands, but at other times, we don't use their names at all? There is a simple reason for this: When you want the dog to move with you in heelwork or come to you when you call him, it is best for you to use the dog's name. After all, when he was a little puppy, his name was about the first word he learned; whenever he heard his name, he understood that you wanted him to follow or come to you. So by using the dog's name with these moving exercises, it helps you and your dog. But when you command the dog to sit, stand, lie down and stay, you don't use his name. If you used his name when telling him to sit, stand or lie down/drop during heelwork, he would quite likely turn half around to you on hearing his name and would then sit, stand or lie down in a crooked position. And if you used his name when telling him to stay, he would likely move off with you. So remember, use the dog's name with exercises of movement, but don't use his name with stationary exercises. You will have noticed that when you did the left turn, you didn't use his name. That was because you made him stop for a fraction of a second.

Do this on the leash first. Tell your dog to "Stay!" Turn around to face him on the full length of a slack leash; call him— "Sam, come!"—and praise him—"Good dog!"—as soon as he takes his first step toward you. Walk backward slowly, praising him all the time, then gather in the leash to sit him and praise him just as you did when you taught him to come while walking.

You really are joining all the exercises together now, aren't you? It makes it more interesting for both of you, and your dog will wonder what is coming next. Great fun, isn't it?

Another piece of advice I wish to give you all, and it is advice I have rarely seen given in dog training books, is to pay particular attention to the finer details in training your dogs.

To do this, remember that your eyesight is your number one resource—I cannot stress that enough. With your eyes on the job, ensure that you use your hands and leash correctly. Pay particular attention to your footwork and body positioning. Use the appropriate intonation, volume, speed and timing of your voice. Think carefully, prepare well, coordinate everything accurately and develop the correct timing with everything you do, especially your voice.

Handlers who do just the bare essentials somehow have the idea that they are good enough. But are they? What happens when something goes wrong, or what if the dog does something wrong or far too slowly, has to be nagged at or, worse still, just stands there and looks at you utterly confused? Whose fault is it? In nearly every case, it is the handler who is at fault. He or she has either said the wrong word, done the wrong action, not corrected the dog nor praised the dog at the right time, left a vital part out, tried to be clever in cutting corners, been inconsistent, not given the dog a good foundation in the training, expected too much, possibly overtrained the dog and made him mentally tired or made many other mistakes and errors like these.

Quite often I have seen handlers, even ones I have instructed for weeks, who report that their dogs are not responding as they should, or as they have in the past. The handlers come to see me again and I give them some basic heelwork for about two minutes.

In that short time and distance in which they walk, I notice a few, and sometimes several, small errors. Because they have not paid attention to detail, they have become very lax and complacent. Their dogs have been smart enough to know that they can get away with careless responses, and have naturally lost respect for their respective handlers. I then work their dogs myself and they work perfectly. Why? It is because I watch and pay particular attention to the finer details. The result is this: The dog knows immediately that I have him under control, that I will not give into him in any way and that I will praise him most sincerely on every good response he makes. All this wins respect from the dog for me. The handler who is watching sees quite clearly how well the dog can work for me, and that the dog certainly has not forgotten any of his work. The handler is often quick to realize that the dog is not at fault, but that his or her handling has become sloppy.

To quickly remedy all this, it is just a simple case of giving the handler refresher-course training. Once this has been done, the dog respects the owner and the good work is restored. I advise the owner to be consistent with everything and to pay attention to even the smallest of details, as they are vitally important. When this is done, the handler should have no more difficulty.

Finally, I urge dog owners not to use food as a reward in training. This may surprise a number of people, but I say it most advisedly and most sincerely.

The food-reward business crept into dog training several years ago and now appears to have taken a stronger following.

In my honest opinion, dog owners are being conned into thinking that it is a very nice, gentle way of training a dog without compulsion. Sure, many dogs will do anything for a piece of food if they are hungry, and some always are! But they are not doing it out of respect for their owner. They are just doing it to get the food. This poses many problems. I grieve for dog owners who come to me, show me their problems and tell me that they have been somewhere else where they were taught to train with food.

My simple answer to their problem is, "Please don't worry. Forget all you've been taught before. Let's start again. With all the exercises, we will show the dog what to do, praise him when he responds, encourage him when he is unsure or lacks willingness and correct him when and where necessary. Everything will be all right, and you will win the respect and affection of the dog, who will then be willing to work with you." That is the basis of good dog training.

Chapter 17
FUN & GAMES

You have seen how enjoyable dog training can be for both you and your dog. The exercises you have learned, particularly the heelwork and the come command, will give you a super start. You might like to leave it there, and if you do, that is quite all right. On the other hand, you might like to learn more. If you do, why not join an obedience dog training class? You will, in time, learn how to do many more exercises, and later you might like to enter your dog into obedience competitions.

When you have taught your dog the basic obedience exercises, why not teach him a few tricks? You'll find that it is great fun, as will your dog, and people watching will get a great thrill.

Shaking Hands

When your dog has learned to sit for his meal and to stay until told that he can eat, you can train him to shake hands. You could either say, "Give me your paw!" or, "Shake hands!" Then lift his front paw up and gently shake it a couple of times. Praise him and then say, "Now the other paw!" and take his other paw in your other hand and give that a couple of gentle shakes, too.

By doing this every time you get your dog to sit for his meals, he will soon learn to shake hands, so well in fact that you won't have to lift his paw up. He will lift it up himself every time you say, "Give me your paw!" You will also find that he will give you the paw that is nearest to your hand. Then ask for the other paw by putting your other hand to the opposite side. Later, the dog will give you his paw at any time of the day; then you can make it one of his little tricks by getting him to shake hands with other people.

Retrieving

If your dog likes carrying something in his mouth or likes running after something and bringing it back to you, then encourage him to do so. Treat it as a great game. If your dog doesn't like doing it, don't worry. There are plenty of other enjoyable things you can do together, and I shall talk about those when we train the dog to do tricks. Teaching the retrieve exercise to a dog who isn't a natural retriever can be very difficult for you and requires much patience. So that exercise is best left for adults to teach the dog.

However, let's imagine your dog likes going after the article you have thrown, but when he picks up the object, he doesn't want to come back to you again! You could be disappointed, but don't worry. Put your dog on a leash, throw the article just a few yards in front of you and say "Fetch!" As the dog goes out to fetch, go with him on the full length of the leash. As soon as the dog picks up the item, praise him joyfully and call him to you just like you did when you were teaching him to come. When you have gotten the dog to sit in front of you, take hold of the article, say "Give!" and as soon as the dog opens his mouth, praise him—"Good dog!"

Shaking hands is one little trick you can teach your dog, especially when you feed him.

Finding a Hidden Article

When and if your dog retrieves quite well, you can go one step further with the game: Tell him to "Sit!" and "Stay!" and then, walking forward a few steps, hide his favorite retrieve article (it might be an old sock, glove or piece of wood) behind something. The dog will know that you have hidden it somewhere, although he cannot see exactly where. Return to your dog's right side and encourage him to "Find!" Off he will trot up to the spot using his nose this time to find it. As soon as the dog picks it up, give praise and call him to you. You can have a lot of fun with

Retrieve: Having thrown the article and said, "Fetch!" praise the dog as soon as he picks up the article and call him to you with continued praise.

this. It is just like the retrieve, but in this case, he has to use his nose to find the hidden article.

Jumping Over a Small Jump

A simple way to teach your dog to go over a small jump is to prop up a board on its edge with some bricks. With your dog at heel on the leash, walk toward the board and say in an excited voice, "Over!" As soon as he jumps over with you, praise him by saying, "Good dog!" Walk on a few more steps, turn around and come back over the jump again. Do it about twice each way for a few days and your dog will soon learn what the word "Over!" means. In the house, you could place a board across a doorway so that there is only one possible way to go over and return. You can do this off the leash, but when you do it, choose a doorway

*Jumping over a board: With your dog at heel on the leash, walk over the board,
saying "Over!" and praise the dog as he jumps.*

that is carpeted on both sides so that your dog can get a good
grip on the ground. Do not do it on a shiny floor, otherwise
the dog might slip, which could put the dog off jumping in
the future.

Now place a low stool at the side of the doorway, sit on it
and rest your leg along the top of the board so that your foot is
against the opposite side of the doorway. Having put the dog in
the sit-stay position inside the room to your left, say "Over!" and
wave your right arm up and over to your right to entice the dog
over your leg. Praise him as he jumps over, then call him "Over!"
again, this time using your left arm up and over to your left.
When the dog hears the second command, "Over!" he should
turn around and take another leap over your leg. Praise the dog
as he jumps.

*Jumping over your leg: Sitting with one leg along a board in a doorway, say "Over!"
and wave your arm up and over to entice the dog over your leg.*

There now, how did you do with that? That was something
new and exciting, wasn't it? Not only was the dog jumping over
the board, but he was leaping over your leg, too. All you had to
do was sit there, give the commands, use your arms to encourage
the dog over and praise him.

Later, you should be able to stand on one leg, hold the
other out straight and, provided your dog is tall enough to jump
that high, say "Over!" Remember, if the dog jumps from your
left, use your right hand to encourage him over your leg.

Jumping Through a Hoop

This is a very simple trick for you to teach your dog. Join the two
ends of a piece of hose pipe together so that it is about the size

It helps if you put your foot against a wall so you can keep your balance.

of a bicycle wheel. With your dog on the leash in a sit-stay position, hold the top of the hoop with your left hand and hold the leash, which is threaded through the hoop, in your right hand. Say "Through!" and encourage your dog to walk through the hoop on a short length of leash. Put your head down so that you can see your dog through the hoop and he can see you. As the dog walks through, praise him, then repeat the exercise about two more times.

You could also teach the dog this trick by holding the hoop in a doorway. As time goes on, you can start holding the hoop a

Jumping through a hoop: Start by teaching the dog to walk on the leash through the hoop with much praise as he walks through.

Every day, gradually put your arms further around the hoop.

little higher off the ground. You can also make the hoop gradually smaller and start putting your arms around the hoop until they nearly meet. By this time, your dog is not only jumping through the hoop, but through your arms as well. Finally, you can do away with the hoop if you want to and just get your dog to jump through your arms. When you call your dog by saying, "Through!" put your head down a bit so that he can see your face through your arms, but as the dog leaps to come through, move your head out of the way.

Finally, when your dog can jump through your arms and hoop, try the trick without the hoop.

Try forming a hoop shape bending your left arm with fingertips just touching your left knee. Say "Through!" and encourage your dog through with your right hand.

Another similar trick is for you to kneel on your right knee and make a hoop by bending your left arm with your fingertips just touching your left knee. Say "Through!" and encourage your dog through the hoop shape with your right hand. Of course, being able to do this depends on how big your dog is and how big you are. However, you should find it quite easy with small- to medium-size dogs. Tiny dogs can also do these tricks, but you must keep everything low to the ground.

Tricks Involving Other People

Another little trick you can do with your dog—and you can invite your friends to help you with it—is to get your dog to jump through and over their arms. Let me show you how to do this.

Ask two friends if they would face each other and each bend down on one knee and hold each other by the hands to form a large hoop. Sit your dog a few steps away facing them. Tell him to stay and then stand on the other side of your two friends, so that your dog can see you through the hoop made with their arms. Call your dog, "Through!" and entice him with your hand. Praise him as he jumps through.

You can also get your dog to jump over their arms if they kneel and hold each other's hands out straight. Ask them to hold their arms down low to start with so that your dog does not run underneath. This time, you should use the word of command, "Over!" Your dog will soon learn the meaning of the words "Through!" and "Over!" I'm sure you will find that your dog will really love doing these tricks; a lot of dogs love showing off to people who visit your home. When your dog has had quite a bit of practice at those jumps, you could get four friends to help you. Ask two to form a hoop and the other two to hold hands outstretched. Have a short distance between each jump. Tell your dog to "Stay!" Position yourself on the other side of your friends so that your dog can see you straight through the center. Call your dog by saying, "Through!" with the first jump and "Over!" with the second. There now, did you enjoy doing those jumps? There doesn't seem to be any end to what you can teach your dog, does there? You are now putting your obedience and tricks together; provided you use the right words of command at the right time, your dog should understand exactly what you want.

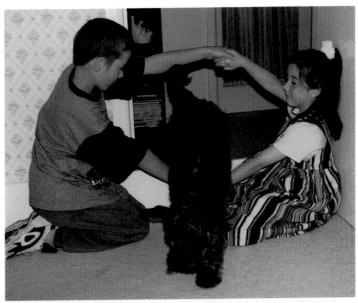

*Jumping through your arms: It is quite a good idea to start this trick
in a doorway indoors on a carpeted area.*

*Jumping over your arms: It is best to have the board to prevent
the dog from running under your arms.*

Having jumped through two pairs of arms, the dog jumps over two more pairs. You could do it again from the opposite direction. This time you will need to say "Over!" for the first jump and "Through!" for the second.

Remember, if you don't use the right words, your dog will either make mistakes or become totally confused, which I'm sure you will agree are terrible things, aren't they?

Remember also, if you forget to praise your dog when he obeys, he may lose interest and either walk away or lie down and refuse to do anything.

Nearly all the games and tricks you can teach your dog are based on basic obedience. However, there is another way a dog can be taught to do something that is based on a natural physical action he makes himself.

Many years ago, my parents owned a lovely tri-colored Border Collie. Whenever he got out of his bed in the morning, or at other times of the day, he would stretch his back legs, then bow down to stretch his front legs with his hindquarters and tail sticking up in the air. As the dog made these two actions, my parents said, "Bow!" when he was about to do the second action. This went on for several weeks; after that, they could tell him to "Bow!" at any time of the day and he was always happy to oblige and bow gracefully.

Years before that we had a Border Collie cross. He was loved by everyone and loved entertaining the crowds of people when our dog training society put on demonstrations of obedience and tricks at various carnivals and festivals in the south of England.

From the time he was a puppy, he often tried to chase his tail. Most times he actually got hold of it and would stand still holding it. Fortunately, he would let go of it when told to do so. Whenever we saw the first sign of his intention to grab his tail, we would say, "Get your tail!" After several weeks, we could say at any time of the day, "Bobbie, get your tail!" and he would get it. Later, we would tell him to come and he came still holding his tail in his mouth until told to "Give!" whereupon he would let go of it. Naturally, we praised him on every response he made and he thought the whole thing was great fun.

I trained him for, and often competed in, obedience competitions, which he also enjoyed. I trained him to do all the obedience exercises laid down by the British Kennel Club. One of the more advanced exercises was, and still is, the send-away, drop and recall. In this exercise, the dog has to be sent away in a straight line to a spot indicated by the judge and commanded to drop. The handler is then required to proceed forward and walk around the dog. When a fair distance away, the handler is told to call his dog to heel. When the dog has raced up to join his handler at heel, both continue forward until told to halt.

Well, I decided to use the first part of that exercise, add the trick to it and finish it off with a novice recall and retrieve.

So one day I sent him away in a straight line down the center of our grass tennis court. Instead of telling him to drop, which he would have expected, I said to him, "Bobbie, get your tail!" This he did and I praised him immediately. I then said, "Come, bring your tail here!" He was very happy to do this, and I praised him all the way. After he reached me, I took hold of his tail, said "Give!" and praised him as soon as he let go; finally, I dismissed him.

Several weeks later something else developed. I noticed that when he took hold of his tail in his mouth, he hung his front paw over his tail while he stood on three legs. Not knowing what he would do, I called him. Would you believe he came to me on three legs with the fourth still hanging over his tail! "I've got a real comic of a dog here," I thought. "What is he going to think of next?"

It was not long after that that he performed this special act at several demonstrations. I briefed our commentator beforehand, and when he announced that the next dog to perform a trick would be sent away and would bring his tail back in his mouth on three legs to his handler, people in the audiences found it very hard to believe until they actually saw it happen. Well, it certainly received a round of applause every time he did it.

Dogs who can do these special acts are rare. Many dog trainers like myself will openly declare that when they look back over the years and recall that among the many dogs they have trained, the dog who had a special aptitude was one in thousands, and they know that they might never have such a dog again. But it is lovely to remember them and the enjoyment they gave to so many people who watched them perform.

In recent years, I had a German Shepherd called Jade. From the time she was a puppy she loved to roll over and lie on her back. She would often do this and play quietly with a tennis ball in her mouth. Every now and then she would take it out of her mouth and hold it between her front paws, look at it and put it back in her mouth again, and all this time she was lying on her back.

Whenever I saw the signs of her going to roll over on her back, I would say, "Roll over on your back!" After many months I was able to get her to do this more or less at any time of the day just by saying, "Roll over on your back!" She just loved doing it.

One day I gave a talk and demonstration with her to the Church of England Boys Society in Melbourne. It was a large, appreciative audience. After I had shown them so many things that she could do, I asked for questions from the audience. After I answered many very intelligent questions, one young boy asked me, "Can your dog roll over on her back?" I detected from the tone in his voice and the way in which he asked the question that he wanted to find out if there was something that the dog could *not* do. I quietly replied, "Yes!" and said no more. There was silence for a moment. Then he said, "Let's see her do it then." Jade was about one yard to my left lying down facing the boy in the front row. I said to her, "Roll over on your back!" As always, she did this without much effort, and she looked at the boy upside down! After several seconds I dismissed her and allowed her to relax. The young boy looked so amazed. I guess it took him and the rest of the boys very much by surprise. "Is there anything else you'd like me to ask my dog to do?" I asked casually. "No, thank you!" the young boy replied quietly.

It is so nice to think about the happy and interesting times we have had with our dogs; the stories I could tell are too numerous to include in this book. Nevertheless, I always like to share these stories with you so that you can appreciate the amount of work that goes into training dogs and their owners and the great rewards that are reaped later by so many.

Chapter 18
TO CONCLUDE

When training with your dog, make everything simple so that your dog can understand. Pay attention to detail and really show the dog what you want. Your eyesight is the most important resource you have when training. Keep your eyes constantly on your dog. Be accurate in everything you do and you will develop good techniques. Your dog will then learn extremely well. Be patient and consistent. Enjoy training and make it a pleasure for your dog.

When training, wear comfortable clothes, but nothing floppy or baggy that is likely to flap around in the wind and disturb the dog. Study your dog and try to understand what he's thinking and what he will probably do if he is distracted. The correct positioning of your hands, feet and body are very important. Develop good vocal control, using different intonations according to what you are teaching your dog. Express your sincere pleasure in the tone of your voice when you praise your dog. Be sure to give him plenty of breaks in training so that he can relax mentally. Never overtrain—the dog is an animal, not a machine!

Very concisely, that is quite a long list of points you will need to follow and adopt in order to make a great success of your dog

Relaxation periods are important for your dog.

training. But I also believe that before anyone starts training a dog, he or she needs to have a positive attitude toward training, not a negative one.

For example, whenever I see a client arrive at my dog training school and get his or her dog out of the car on a leash and walk up my drive to meet me for the first time, I say to myself, "Here comes another person and dog and I am going to train them. It doesn't matter what problems they may have, nor the various methods I will need to use, I will train them together." That is a positive attitude.

Imagine me saying to myself quite the opposite: "Here comes another person and dog, but I doubt very much if I will be able to do anything with them even if I do try. I don't have much hope for either of them." That is a negative attitude; no one will achieve anything that way.

Although most people have a positive attitude, others, unfortunately, have a negative one. After I show them how to perform an exercise and invite them to do it themselves, they will say, "Oh! I know I'll never be able to do that," or, "My dog might do it for you, but I know that he certainly won't do it for me!"

With these people I have to say, "Please! Never, never say you can't do something. If you do, you are acting like a defeatist before you even start. Instead, I would like to hear you say, 'Well, I can see how well my dog works for you, now let me try it.' When you have said that, I know that you are enthusiastic to train your dog and get good results."

We all have to accept the fact that certain breeds are not as easy to train as others, and a few may even be regarded as being more or less impossible! Oh, you may be able to teach them something, but they will not perform with any reliability. Putting all breeds into five main groups, you will find that all the sheep herding breeds are the most receptive. All the retrieving breeds come a very close second in their working ability. The third group is all the terriers—they are all trainable but are not so easy. The fourth group contains all the hounds, and they are generally most difficult to train. The fifth group is extremely difficult; even when you have trained them to do a few simple exercises, you cannot trust them—they are most unreliable. It doesn't matter how much experience you have had as a dog trainer; you have to accept the fact that those few breeds do not lend themselves to training. This last group would include breeds such as the Chow Chow, Basenji and a few others.

Throughout your training you have to try to think like a dog and understand how he sees you. When you can do this, you will be able to see more clearly how his mind works.

To give you a clear example of this, let us have another look at the dismissal command and signal with both hands in Chapter 14. I say something like, "Go free!" or, "Off you go and play!" and at the same time give a signal from under the dog's chin by spreading both of my hands forward and outward down the path.

The two hands signal, or gesture if you like, helps the dog to understand that the phrase means that the lesson is over and now he can relax. While most people follow these instructions with success, others use the hand signal from the middle of their own waist; because the dog does not notice the movement of the handler's hands, he remains in the sit position.

To help the handlers understand this I ask them to imagine they are dogs! I stand on their right, ask them to look straight ahead, put my hands above their heads and cast my hands forward and outward. As I do this, I ask, "Can you see my hands?" "No, I can't!" is the reply. I then put both of my hands just beneath their chins and cast them forward and outward and ask, "Can you see my hands this time?" "Yes!" they reply. "Can you understand now why it is necessary to put your hands just under the point of your dog's chin so that he can see and understand what you are permitting him to do?" A simple visual instructional technique like this helps handlers to see it from their own dog's angle and develop a greater and deeper understanding of their dogs.

It is truly amazing what we can do in training dogs in a step-by-step process. I shall always remember the kind words said by a blind lady whom I trained with a guide dog many years ago. She was a physiotherapist, and at the graduation party held at the guide dog training center, she paid tribute to all the staff and the instruction given during the four-week course. She said, "When I came here and was given a brief outline of what we were all going to do with our guide dogs, who had been highly trained for months before, I found it beyond my imagination and comprehension that we would achieve so much in one month. But now we have all found that that has become a reality. All the stages of training have been so gradually fed to us that we have hardly noticed how much we have achieved. All the training has been cleverly thought out."

I think those last few words certainly sum up any dog training program, don't they? Another compliment that I will always remember with appreciation was made by a blind man who had just finished training with his first guide dog. He said, "Whenever anything went wrong, our instructors would say, 'Don't worry! Let's have another try. You will get it!' And sure enough we did. Such encouraging words put us at ease and restored our confidence."

Well, I hope you have found all I have had to say in this book both interesting and helpful. Whatever dog you choose, care for him and train him well. Love your dog and enjoy his companionship. When you do all these things, you will be rewarded more than you would ever have imagined. Good luck!

Index